THE ULTIMATE WORLD OF DINOSAURS

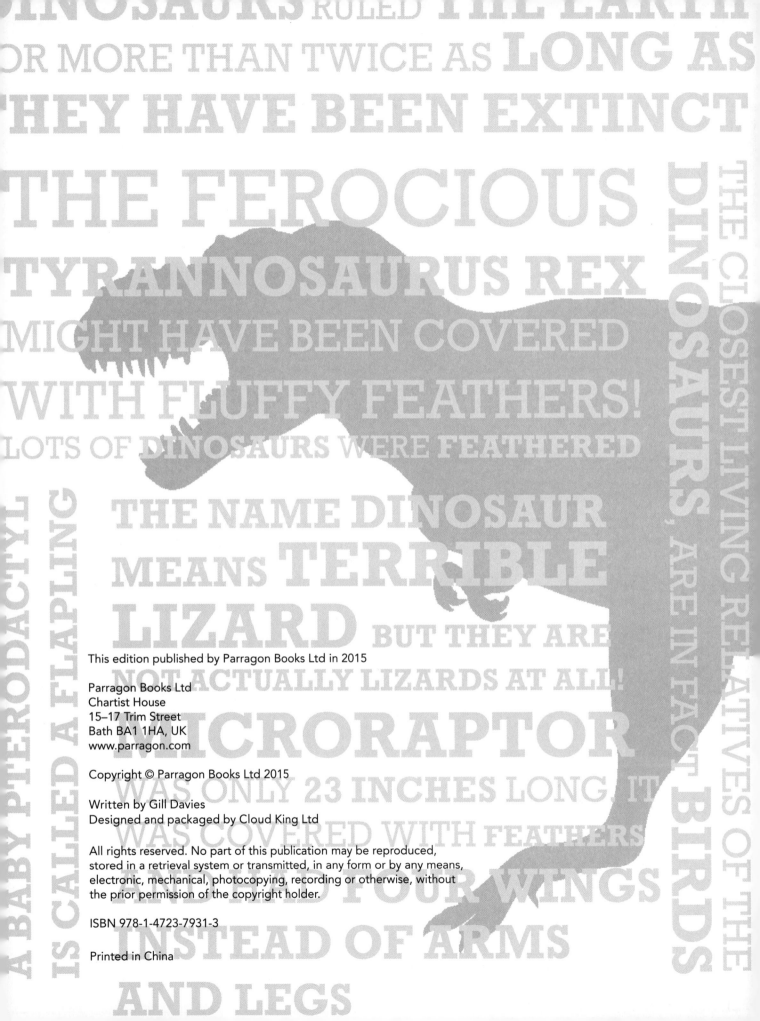

This edition published by Parragon Books Ltd in 2015

Parragon Books Ltd
Chartist House
15–17 Trim Street
Bath BA1 1HA, UK
www.parragon.com

Copyright © Parragon Books Ltd 2015

Written by Gill Davies
Designed and packaged by Cloud King Ltd

ISBN 978-1-4723-7931-3

Printed in China

THE ULTIMATE WORLD OF DINOSAURS

PaRragon

Bath • New York • Cologne • Melbourne • Delhi
Hong Kong • Shenzhen • Singapore • Amsterdam

CONTENTS

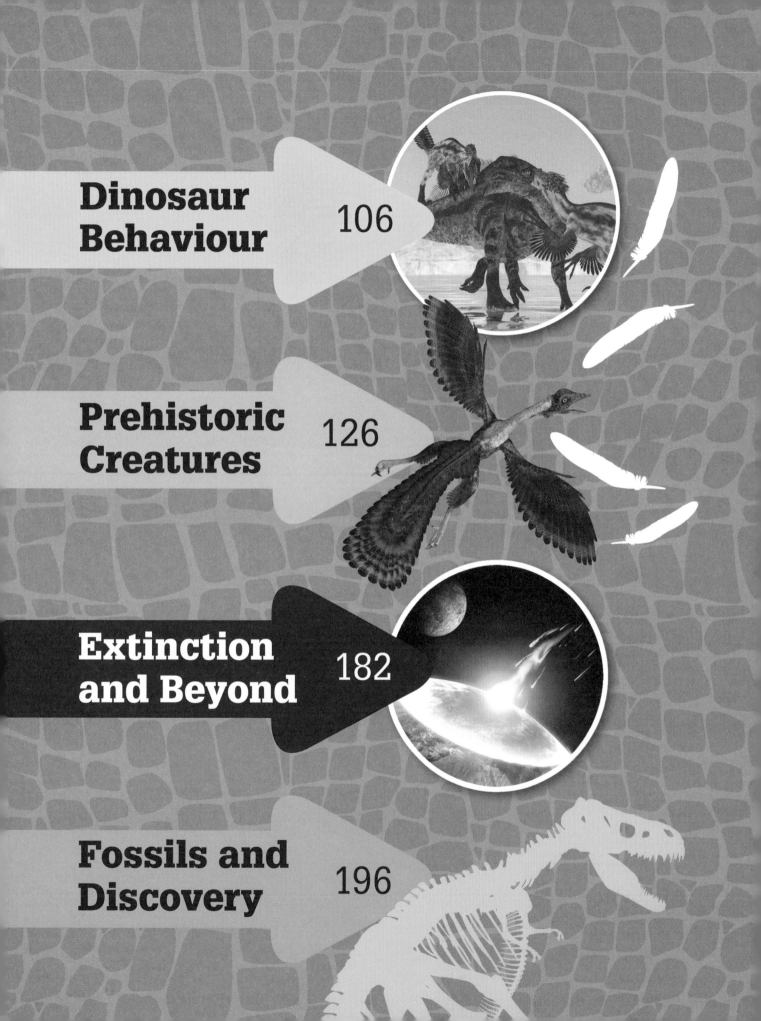

THE
DINOSAUR
WORLD

CHAPTER 1

Dinosaurs are among the **MOST AMAZING** creatures ever.

They roamed Earth for more than 160 million years – that's **820 times longer** than modern humans have existed.

#0001

FACTS ABOUT
8 BEING A DINOSAUR

THE WORD *DINOSAUR* MEANS
"TERRIBLE LIZARD",
but although dinosaurs were
reptiles, they were **NOT** actually lizards!

#0002

Dinosaurs
lived on Earth
during the
Mesozoic Era,
252 to 66 million
years ago.

#0003

DINOSAURS may
have been the most
SUCCESSFUL creatures
ever to live on

EARTH.

#0004

SOME DINOSAURS were as small as a chicken;

others were BIGGER than a truck.

#0005

The flying **pterosaurs** and swimming **plesiosaurs** of the Mesozoic Era were **NOT dinosaurs.**

#0006

Some dinosaurs ate only **plants**; others hunted or scavenged for **meat.**

#0007

DINOSAURS WERE LAND ANIMALS, ALTHOUGH SOME **EVOLVED INTO BIRDS.**

#0008

Unlike today's lizards and crocodiles, whose legs stick out from the sides of their bodies, a dinosaur's pillar-like legs were set **DIRECTLY BENEATH IT.**

#0009

9

8 FACTS ABOUT PLANET DINOSAUR

When dinosaurs first lived on Earth, there was just one GIGANTIC **supercontinent. Called PANGAEA,** it was the only land mass within a vast ocean. #0010

The climate of **Pangaea** was **HOT** and **DRY.** #0011

Pangaea formed an **INCREDIBLE 300 TO 270 MILLION YEARS AGO.** #0012

The name **Pangaea** comes from the Greek words "pan" and "gaia", which mean "Mother Earth". #0013

Pangaea covered almost **ONE-THIRD** of Earth's surface, just as the continents do today.

#0014

The one **VAST global ocean** surrounding Pangaea was **named Panthalassa.**

#0015

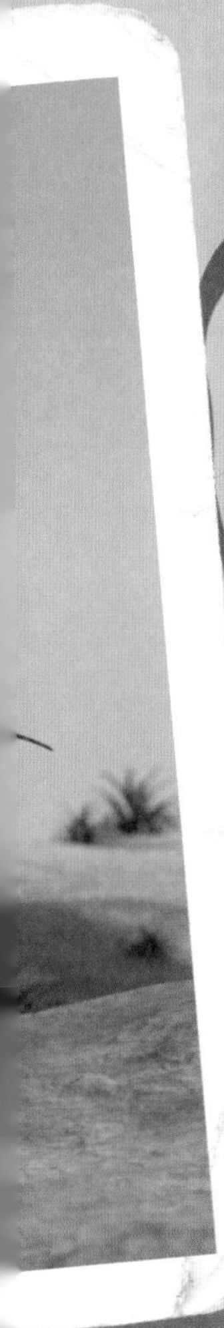

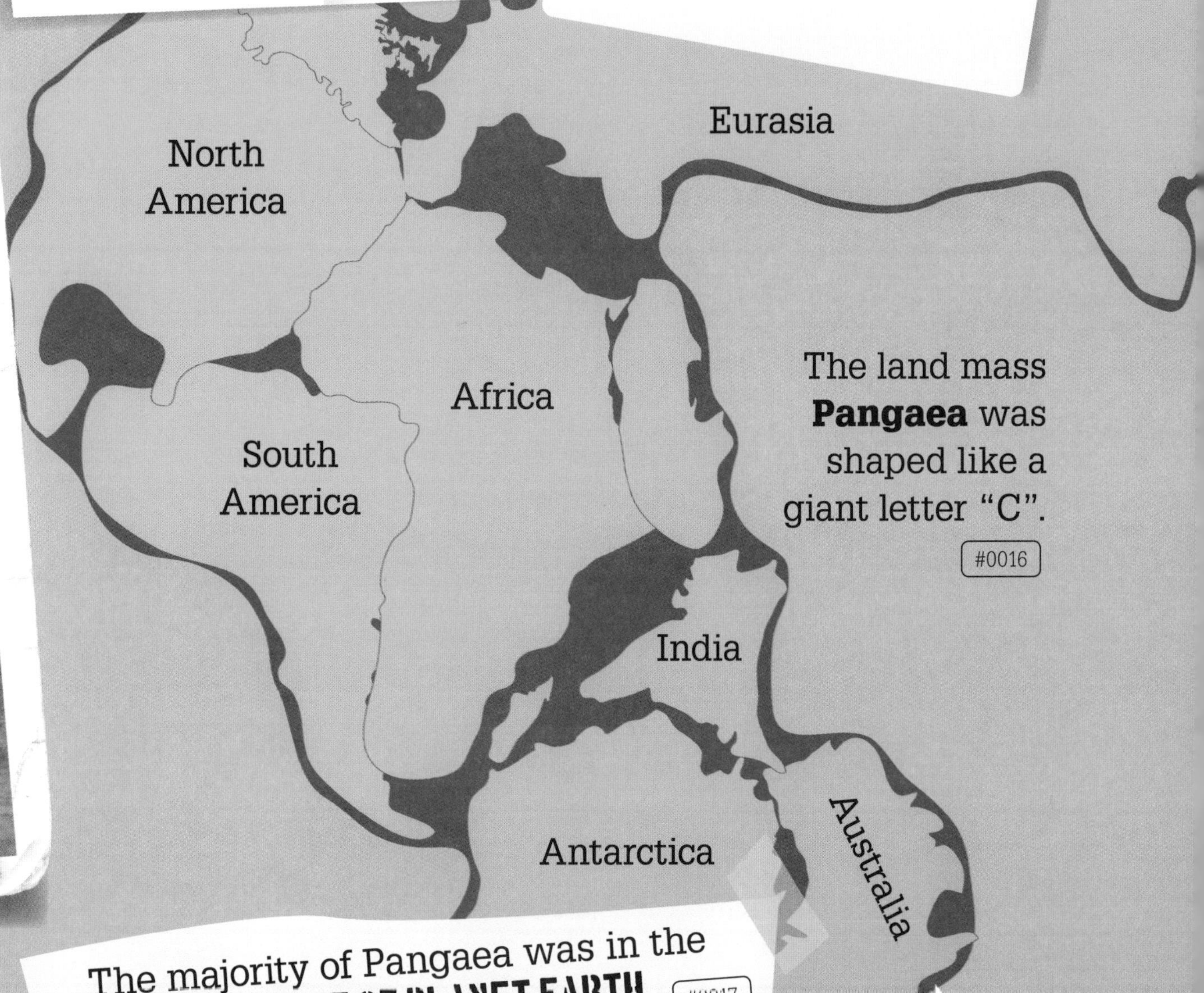

Eurasia

North America

Africa

South America

The land mass **Pangaea** was shaped like a giant letter "C".

#0016

India

Antarctica

Australia

The majority of Pangaea was in the **SOUTHERN HALF OF PLANET EARTH.** #0017

7 FACTS ABOUT THE CHANGING WORLD

Laurasia
North America
Eurasia
Gondwana
South America
Africa
India
Tethys Ocean
Antarctica
Australia

About **175 MILLION YEARS AGO,** Pangaea began to break up into **two new SUPERCONTINENTS** – Laurasia and Gondwana.

#0018

As Pangaea broke up, vast rifts between the continents created

NEW oceans and seas.

#0019

The new continents brought huge climate changes. #0020

For a while, **LAURASIA** and **GONDWANA** were linked by land.
#0021

DINOSAURS CROSSED

over the land between the two supercontinents. #0022

As the **climates** across the continents **changed,** the **variety** of dinosaurs, plants and other animals **increased.**
#0023

By the end of the Mesozoic Era, **Earth's land masses** had separated to become today's seven continents.
#0024

13

11 FACTS ABOUT THE
DINOSAUR TIMELINE

The Mesozoic Era, the age of the dinosaurs, is divided into three periods: the Triassic, Jurassic and Cretaceous. #0025

MASS EXTINCTIONS

are caused by vast ice sheets, volcanic eruptions, earthquakes or asteroids slamming into Earth. #0026

The first **DINOSAURS**, mammals and crocodilians appeared in the Triassic. #0027

TRIASSIC
252 to 201 million years ago

Reptiles, such as rhynchosaurs, **DOMINATED** the land during the Triassic. #0028

JURASSIC
201 to 145 million years ago

CRETACEOUS
145 to 66 million years ago

Jurassic plants included ferns, cycads, rushes and conifers, which all provided **FOOD** for the dinosaurs.

#0029

During the Jurassic, **dinosaurs EXPANDED** into many new habitats.

#0030

Ammonites flourished in the **Jurassic** seas.

#0032

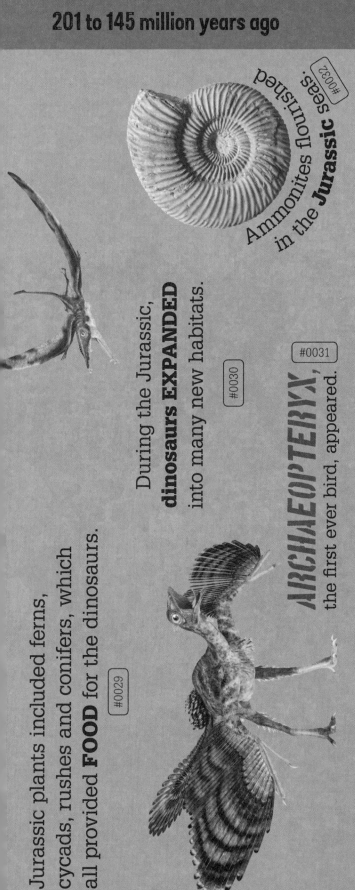

ARCHAEOPTERYX, the first ever bird, appeared.

#0031

At the end of the Cretaceous, there was a **MASS EXTINCTION,** and most of the dinosaurs died out.

#0034

About 16 PER CENT of ocean species died out at the end of the Cretaceous.

#0035

There were more **kinds** of dinosaur in the **Cretaceous** than ever before, including the horned **CERATOPSIANS.**

#0033

15

FACTS ABOUT THE
9 TRIASSIC PERIOD

The very **FIRST** dinosaurs appeared in the middle of the **Triassic.** #0036

The Triassic lasted
51 MILLION YEARS,

from 252 to 201 million years ago. #0037

For some of the
TRIASSIC,
it was so hot that vast, baking deserts stretched across the land. #0038

The
TRIASSIC OCEANS
were filled with creatures such as **ammonites** and large **sea reptiles** called ichthyosaurs.

#0039

Triassic **polar regions** were covered with **lush forests** rather than snow and ice.
#0040

There were no birds, but the **Triassic skies** were filled with **flying reptiles** called pterosaurs.
#0041

The first mammals appeared towards the end of the **TRIASSIC.**
#0042

The **TRIASSIC CLIMATE** was generally **warmer** than today.
#0043

Throughout the whole of the Triassic, there were no flowering plants and
#0044 **NO GRASS.**

12 FACTS ABOUT THE JURASSIC PERIOD

The Jurassic lasted for **56 million years.** #0045

The Jurassic began **201 million years ago** and ended **145 million years ago.** #0046

The vast Jurassic forests were full of tall tree ferns, ginkgoes, giant horsetails, mosses, pines and many other conifer trees. #0047

THE JURASSIC SEAS WERE FULL of ichthyosaurs, horseshoe crabs, plesiosaurs, giant crocodile-like creatures, sharks, rays and ammonites. #0048

A few early shrew-like mammals crept about in the Jurassic foliage. #0049

HUGE sauropods, such as *DIPLODOCUS*...

Sturdy Jurassic stegosaurs, such as *Stegosaurus*, had **BODY PARTS** that they could use in their defence, such as tail spikes. #0050

18

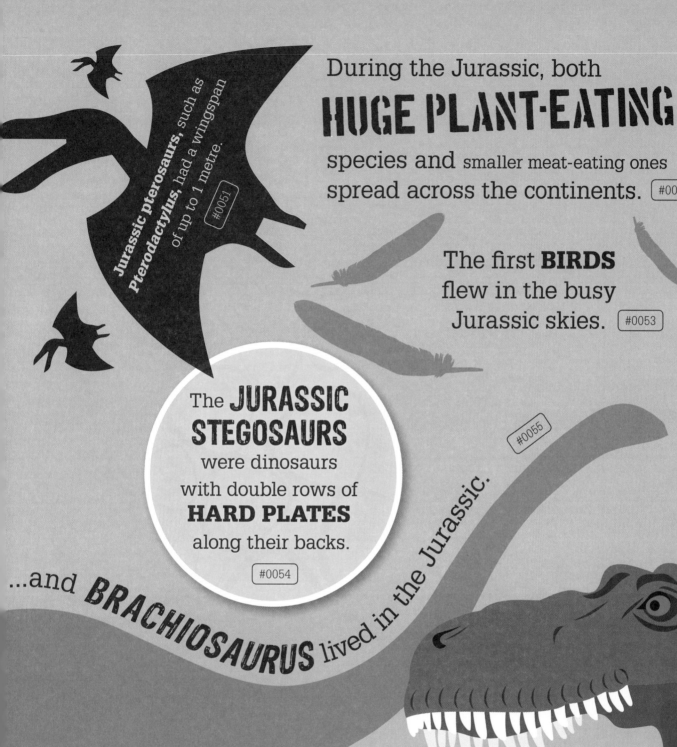

Jurassic pterosaurs, such as Pterodactylus, had a wingspan of up to 1 metre. #0051

During the Jurassic, both **HUGE PLANT-EATING** species and smaller meat-eating ones spread across the continents. #0052

The first **BIRDS** flew in the busy Jurassic skies. #0053

The **JURASSIC STEGOSAURS** were dinosaurs with double rows of **HARD PLATES** along their backs. #0054

...and **BRACHIOSAURUS** lived in the Jurassic. #0055

Allosaurus was a mean, **DANGEROUS** Jurassic dinosaur that fed on stegosaurs and sauropods. #0056

7 FACTS ABOUT THE CRETACEOUS PERIOD

The **Cretaceous** saw the abundance of many animal groups, including **insects, mammals** and **birds**. New dinosaur groups included pachycephalosaurs, ceratopsians and hadrosaurs. #0057

Flowering plants probably first appeared in the **early Cretaceous** and eventually dominated the landscape. #0058

The oldest fossil of a flowering plant is *ARCHAEFRUCTUS LIAONINGENSIS,* which grew in the Cretaceous and is **125 million years old!** #0059

The Cretaceous lasted from **145 to 66 MILLION YEARS ago** and was the longest and last period of the **Mesozoic Era.**

#0060

Cycads, ferns and conifers

grew throughout the Cretaceous. New trees with broad leaves, such as oak, beech and walnut, began to appear as the climate became more varied.

#0061

During the **Cretaceous,** some pterosaurs, such as **Quetzalcoatlus,** had wingspans of up to 9 metres.

#0062

Although the Cretaceous ended with a **mass extinction** of dinosaurs, many flowering plants, mammals and insects lived on.

#0063

FACTS ABOUT
6 DINOSAUR NEIGHBOURS

MINIBEASTS

such as flies, mosquitoes, wasps and bees shared the dinosaur world. #0064

Insects became **TRAPPED IN AMBER,** a sticky resin from trees, and their fossils were **FOUND** millions of years later! #0065

Cretaceous leaf-hoppers jumped from leaf to leaf, sucking sap from trees. #0066

22

Modern bees and wasps first appeared in the Cretaceous. They collected nectar from the new flowering plants. #0067

Tiny ant-like beetles named *Kachinus*, just 0.6 millimetres long, scuttled in the Cretaceous undergrowth.

#0068

INSECTS SCAVENGED DINOSAUR CORPSES. Some of them, such as cockroaches and possibly early types of dung beetle, may have cleared away their droppings. #0069

23

11 FACTS ABOUT DINOSAUR RELATIVES

Dinosaurs were reptiles, but not all reptiles were dinosaurs.
#0070

Scutosaurus was a large Triassic reptile that roamed the floodplains in large herds, probably making **LOUD BELLOWS.**
#0072

Scutosaurus had a *horny head* #0071 protected by **spikes** and **plates.**

Smooth-skinned amphibians evolved into scaly reptiles more than **300 MILLION YEARS AGO.**
#0073

Before dinosaurs took over the land, semi-aquatic creatures called crocodilians were among the most **FEARSOME REPTILES.**

They dominated their water's-edge habitat for more than **200 MILLION YEARS.**
#0074

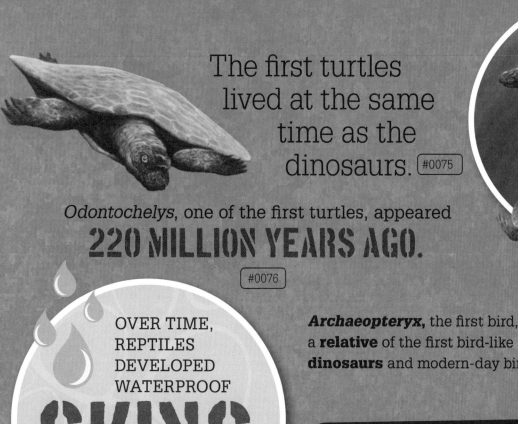

The first turtles lived at the same time as the dinosaurs. #0075

Odontochelys, one of the first turtles, appeared **220 MILLION YEARS AGO.** #0076

OVER TIME, REPTILES DEVELOPED WATERPROOF **SKINS.** #0077

Archaeopteryx, the first bird, is a **relative** of the first bird-like **dinosaurs** and modern-day birds. #0078

During the Mesozoic Era, reptiles began to lay **watertight eggs.** This meant that they could lay their eggs on land. #0079

Most **rhynchosaurs** lived in the **TRIASSIC.** These reptiles had a powerful beak and massive back claws for digging up food from the ground. #0080

DINOSAUR WORLD FACTFILE

The fierce **meat eater** T. REX was one of the **biggest** Cretaceous predators. #0081

Grass-like plants have been found in fossilized **DINOSAUR POO** dating back **65 MILLION YEARS** – 10 million years earlier than they were thought to have grown! #0082

DURING THE CRETACEOUS **EXTINCTION,** DEBRIS FROM AN ASTEROID IMPACT DARKENED THE SKIES AND STARVED THE EARTH OF SUNLIGHT. #0083

PALAEONTOLOGISTS TELL US THAT MANY DINOSAURS WERE COVERED IN #0084

FEATHERS.

Big land dinosaurs **existed on Earth** for **160 MILLION YEARS,** whereas modern **HUMANS** have been around for only **200,000 years.** #0085

Dinosaurs lived in ANTARCTICA as the Poles were ice-free back then. In 1986, their fossils were found there. #0086

Today's crickets have **ancient relatives** that lived at the same time as dinosaurs in the **JURASSIC FORESTS.** #0087

SO FAR, FOSSILS OF AROUND

1000

DIFFERENT TYPES OF DINOSAUR HAVE BEEN DISCOVERED.

#0088

Some **dinosaurs** were similar to modern-day **ostriches,** and perhaps **RAN JUST AS FAST.**

#0089

Not all early mammals were tiny. **REPENOMAMUS** grew to nearly **1 metre long** and **ATE DINOSAURS.**

#0090

BEFORE MUCH WAS KNOWN ABOUT DINOSAURS, THEIR **REMAINS** WERE THOUGHT TO BE THE BONES OF **GIANTS** OR **OGRES.**

#0091

SHARKS

have swum in our oceans for over **400 MILLION years.**

#0092

DINOSAURS are members of a large group of extinct animals that scientists call **DINOSAURIA.**

#0093

In 1824, the first land dinosaur was named **MEGALOSAURUS...**

...nearly **150 years** after its fossil bones were first found!

#0094

DINOSAUR
ANATOMY

Dinosaurs were TOUGH!

Their bodies could recover from injuries and infections that would kill most animals today. #0095

Dinosaurs had straight knees and ankles, which meant they could **STAND** with their **LEGS** directly **BENEATH** their bodies. #0096

12 FACTS ABOUT SIZE

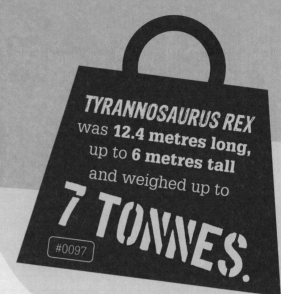

TYRANNOSAURUS REX was **12.4 metres long,** up to **6 metres tall** and weighed up to **7 TONNES.**

#0097

Sauropod dinosaurs, such as Brachiosaurus, were **SO TALL** that they make today's giraffes look **really short!**

#0098

The **largest animal ever** is NOT a dinosaur, but the **blue whale.**

#0099

Camarasaurus was an incredible 18 metres long. #0100

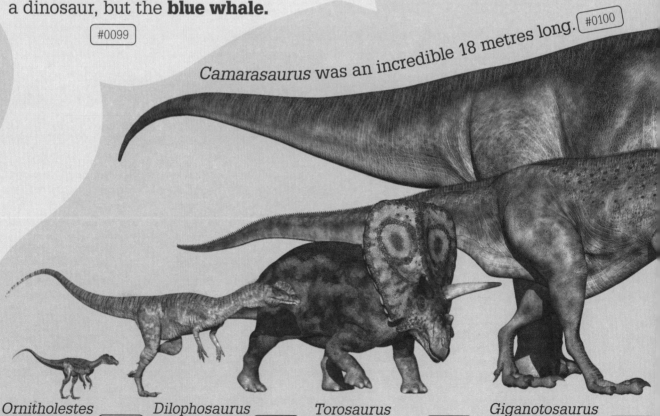

Ornitholestes
2 metres long #0101

Dilophosaurus
6 metres long #0102

Torosaurus
7.5 metres long #0103

Giganotosaurus
12.5 metres long #0104

A baby **Tyrannosaurus rex** was only 3 metres long, but a growth spurt when it was about 14 years old meant it quickly reached full size. #0105

Tyrannosaurus rex was fully grown by the time it was 19 years old.

#0106

It is likely that dinosaurs were warm-blooded rather than cold-blooded as it takes a lot of internal heat to grow quickly.

#0107

Argentinosaurus...

...was longer than three buses lined up end to end.

#0108

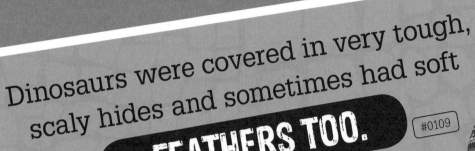

FACTS ABOUT
8 SKIN AND COLOUR

Dinosaurs were covered in very tough, scaly hides and sometimes had soft

FEATHERS TOO.

#0109

The fossil skin impressions left on *Carnotaurus*' fossil bones reveal many disc-like scales.

#0110

The colour and texture of dinosaur skin were, for a long time, completely unknown to the scientists who studied them.

#0111

Carnotaurus' scales were like a mosaic with large pebble-like

BUMPS.

#0112

Scientists believe that Sinosauropteryx was covered in **orange feathers** and...

...had a STRIPED TAIL.

#0113

The dinosaurs that evolved into birds had skin that was much thinner and lighter than non-bird dinosaurs.

#0114

Skin pigments in the fossils of two prehistoric sea reptiles – a

196-MILLION-YEAR-OLD

ichthyosaur and an

86-MILLION-YEAR-OLD

mosasaur – were almost black. This suggested to scientists that dinosaur skin may have been black too.

#0115

Amazingly, fossilized *Anchiornis feathers* have been found containing traces of **COLOUR** pigments, showing that they were black, white and grey.

#0116

9 FACTS ABOUT BODY ARMOUR

Some **DINOSAURS** had large plates of **BONY ARMOUR, SPIKES** AND **CLUBBED TAILS.**

#0117

The first armoured dinosaurs had **BONY SCALES (SCUTES),** just like crocodiles.

#0118

Pentaceratops had **five horns:** a nose horn, two cheek horns and a horn above each eye.

#0119

MIGHTY 2-tonne ankylosaur *Euoplocephalus* had spikes and a **CLUBBED TAIL.** #0120

Euoplocephalus may have swung its tail club from side to side, whacking the legs of larger attacking dinosaurs. #0121

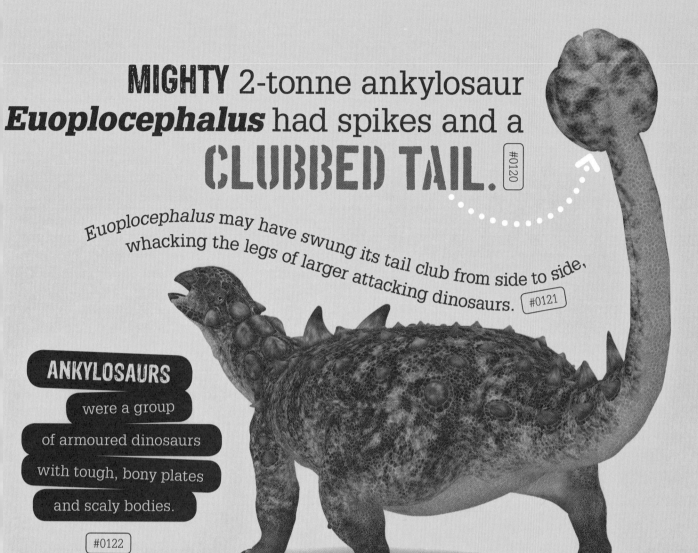

ANKYLOSAURS were a group of armoured dinosaurs with tough, bony plates and scaly bodies.

#0122

Euoplocephalus had **BONY EYELIDS,** which protected its eyes. #0123

Each of *Stegosaurus'* plates were around **75 to 80** centimetres tall.

#0124

Stegosaurus' plates were covered in keratin, the same substance from which human hair is made.

#0125

7 FACTS ABOUT DINOSAUR CLAWS

Therizinosaurus had

GIGANTIC FRONT CLAWS 1 METRE LONG.

#0126

Therizinosaurus used its **claws** when feeding by **grabbing** leafy branches, **stripping** bark from trees and maybe even **tearing open** termite mounds. #0127

Claws may have been displayed to scare off enemies or attract mates. #0128

Some meat-eating dinosaurs, such as *Deinonychus*, had **DEADLY CLAWS**, which they used to slash at their victims.

#0129

The name *Deinonychus* means **"TERRIBLE CLAW"**.

#00130

Deinonychus had a deadly, retractable claw on each foot.

#0131

Some dinosaurs used their claws to kill their prey; others used them to hold down their prey, keeping their victim in a deadly grip before finishing it off with a **FATAL BITE.**

#0132

11 FACTS ABOUT DINOSAUR MOVEMENT

Tyrannosaurus rex could possibly run at **30 kilometres per hour** – that's as fast as a modern-day polar bear can run. #0134

Dinosaurs probably used their **long, stiff tails** for balance as they walked and ran. #0135

Scientists study **FOSSILIZED** dinosaur footprints to work out how **FAST** dinosaurs could **MOVE.** #0136

Compsognathus was a tiny dinosaur that may have been able to reach speeds of more than 60 kilometres per hour. #0137

FOSSILIZED DINOSAUR TRACKS

prove that **dinosaurs walked** with their tails held above the ground. #0138

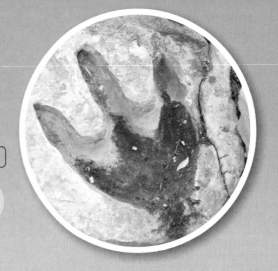

Dinosaurs walked with their toes pointing **inwards.** #0139

Dreadnoughtus, a **MASSIVE** recently discovered dinosaur, left **FOOTPRINTS** the size of washing machines. #0140

LARGE QUADRUPEDAL

(four-legged) dinosaurs, such as *Alamosaurus*, moved slowly at **about 8 kilometres per hour.** #0141

Some of the BIRD-LIKE DINOSAURS may have flapped their feathered arms to help them **move faster.** #0142

Giant sauropods had long, flexible necks so they could feed over a wide area by swinging their necks, and standing still. #0143

11 FACTS ABOUT BIPEDAL DINOSAURS

Many of the **earliest** dinosaurs were bipeds.
#0144

Bipedal dinosaurs walked on **TWO FEET,** not four.
#0145

Theropods were a group of bipedal dinosaurs that included **TOP PREDATORS.**
#0146

Like all raptors, *Utahraptor* was a **SWIFT-RUNNING** biped.
#0147

BIPEDAL DINOSAURS could run farther than most reptiles today.
#0148

While *Spinosaurus* usually **WALKED ON TWO LEGS,** it may have occasionally crouched and rested on all four.
#0149

OTHER BIPEDAL DINOSAURS INCLUDE:
Albertosaurus, Allosaurus, Baryonyx, Eoraptor, Gallimimus, Megalosaurus, Oviraptor and Troodon.

#0150

Bipeds included both **MEAT EATERS** and **PLANT EATERS**, but almost all quadrupedal (four-legged) dinosaurs were plant eaters.

#0151

Some bipedal dinosaur species had arms that, **OVER MILLIONS OF YEARS,** evolved into wings.

#0153

Dinosaurs with **HEAVY** heads, horns and neck frills, such as Triceratops, could not have walked on two legs without toppling over.

#0152

Some meat eaters that walked on two legs used their forelimbs to grab prey, but not *Tyrannosaurus rex* – its arms were much too short!

#0154

41

9 FACTS ABOUT DINOSAUR BRAINS

Scientists study **bird** and **crocodile** brains as a way of better understanding dinosaur brains.
#0155

Dinosaur relative **Archaeopteryx** had enlarged brain regions for control over sight. #0156

Many Triassic **PLANT EATERS** had very small **brains** but a good sense of smell. #0157

Cretaceous plant eaters like *Edmontosaurus* had slightly **bigger brains** than Jurassic plant eaters, but their brains were still smaller than those of the dinosaurs that ate them! #0158

In proportion to its size, **ARCHAEOPTERYX's** brain was similar to the brains of modern-day birds. #0159

42

TROODON

had a **large brain** in relation to its small body, making it probably one of the **smartest dinosaurs.**

#0161

To hunt prey at speed, dinosaurs needed bigger brains. #0160

Velociraptor had a **BIG BRAIN** for its size. It also had excellent eyesight and hearing. #0162

Tyrannosaurus rex had a **BIGGER BRAIN** than any plant eater.

#0163

43

7 FACTS ABOUT TEETH

Duck-billed dinosaurs, called hadrosaurs, had horny, toothless beaks, but up to **1000 cheek teeth** in the sides of their jaws.

#0164

DINOSAUR-EATING

prehistoric crocodiles, found in the Sahara Desert in Africa, included **FEROCIOUS KAPROSUCHUS.**

It had three sets of **DAGGER-SHAPED** fangs for slicing up meat.

#0165

Turkey-sized **Heterodontosaurus,** whose name means "different-tooth lizard", had three kinds of teeth plus a beak. #0166

Heterodontosaurus had **sharp** incisors for
CUTTING,
chisel-like teeth for **grinding** and tusk-like teeth for **DEFENDING ITSELF!** #0167

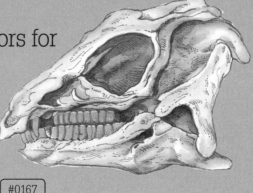

All dinosaurs **replaced lost teeth** by growing new ones. #0168

TYRANNOSAURUS REX'S teeth were as **BIG AS BANANAS,** but a lot harder. They were strong enough to **crush bone.** #0169

Meat-eating dinosaurs such as **TYRANNOSAURUS REX** used their huge, sharp teeth to make a kill, usually by biting the neck of their prey. #0170

45

FACTS ABOUT
11 FEATHERED
DINOSAURS

Feathers helped to insulate dinosaurs and keep them warm.

#0171

In the 1990s, fossil discoveries showed that many **DINOSAURS HAD FEATHERS.**

#0172

One set of fossilized dinosaur feathers contains **beta keratin,** a protein found in modern-day bird feathers.

#0173

Feathers may have first appeared

220 MILLION YEARS AGO

IN THE TRIASSIC PERIOD.

#0174

In the late 1800s, biologist **Thomas Henry Huxley** was the first person to show that birds were the descendants of feathered dinosaurs.

#0175

Feathers were most common among small theropod dinosaurs, such as *Caudipteryx.*

#0176

SOME FOSSILS SHOW
FEATHERS;
others show quill knobs – bumps
where the feathers were attached. #0177

The first fossil of a feathered plant-eating dinosaur was
discovered in 2014. This showed that **BOTH MEAT-EATING
AND PLANT-EATING DINOSAURS** may have had feathers.
#0178

NOT ALL FEATHERED DINOSAURS EVOLVED INTO BIRDS.
#0180

Feathered
dinosaurs existed
for around
100 MILLION YEARS. #0179

About 30 species of

feathered dinosaurs

have been identified.

#0181

FACTS ABOUT
9 BEAKS, BILLS AND CRESTS

Erlikosaurus was a therapod dinosaur with a **HARD SNOUT** that was covered with keratin, just like a bird's beak.
#0182

Erlikosaurus' tough snout may have stopped its skull from being shaken when it battered away at hard food.
#0183

A hadrosaur dinosaur's duckbill was more than half as long as its skull.
#0184

Scientists think that hadrosaur duckbills evolved to replace teeth.
#0185

Ceratopsian dinosaurs, such as *Triceratops*, had small beaks.
#0186

Daspletosaurus' **HUGE HEAD** was probably used to knock its prey unconscious.
#0187

48

A dinosaur's beak was like a multi-tool penknife because it functioned as so many tools in one. It was used for:

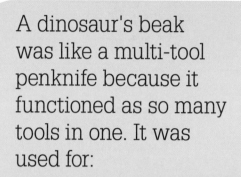

feeding, protection, cleaning and preening. #0188

As well as their **tough duckbills,** some hadrosaurs had a hollow crest on the top of their heads, which made

LOUD HORN BLASTS.

#0189

Crests may have helped **HADROSAURS,** such as *CORYTHOSAURUS,* to recognize each other.

#0190

49

FACTS ABOUT
7 DINOSAUR SIGHT

Dinosaurs probably had **BETTER VISION** than most other prehistoric reptiles.

#0191

Plant eater *Camarasaurus* had **eyes on the sides of its head,** giving it a wide field of vision with which to spot danger.

#0192

Predatory dinosaur *Troodon*

HAD LARGE EYES,

which were probably useful for hunting at **dusk and dawn.**

#0193

50

Deinonychus may have been able to see in the dark.

#0194

Like most of the meat-eating therapods, *Aucasaurus* had **forward-facing** eyes, which helped it to judge the distance to its prey. #0195

BECAUSE SOME DINOSAURS HAD BRIGHT FEATHERS AND CRESTS, SCIENTISTS THINK IT IS POSSIBLE THAT THEY COULD SEE IN COLOUR. #0196

Leaellynasaura probably had good night vision as it lived close to the South Pole, where winter days are short and nights are long. #0197

51

FACTS ABOUT

8 HEARING AND SMELL

MEAT EATERS

didn't only track down live animals. Their **good sense of smell** helped them find dead animals, too.

#0198

All **dinosaurs had ears** with eardrums and inner ears, just as humans do.

#0199

Large plant-eating dinosaurs could hear low-pitched sounds, and small plant eaters high-pitched sounds.

#0200

Plant eaters needed a

GOOD SENSE OF SMELL

to sniff out the best plants to eat.

#0201

Meat-eating dinosaurs used their powerful sense of smell to detect low-flying pterosaurs. #0202

PLANT EATERS

may have used their sense of smell to find a mate. #0203

The 21-metre-long sauropod **JOBARIA** had very large nasal openings and was likely to have had a keen sense of smell. #0204

A dinosaur's **inner ear** was used as much for **BALANCE** as it was for hearing. #0205

8 FACTS ABOUT DINOSAUR POO

Just like bones, **dinosaur poo** became fossilized and survived for **MILLIONS OF YEARS.** #0206

Fossil **poos** are called **coprolites.** #0207

Some **DINOSAUR POO** can tell us which food types a **dinosaur may have eaten.** #0208

Dinosaur poo helped fertilize the soil so that plants could grow, keeping the forests lush and green. #0209

Researchers now think that **cockroaches** ATE DINOSAUR POO. #0210

If sold at auction, **DINOSAUR POO** attracts huge sums of money – even **thousands of pounds.** #0211

Dinosaur coprolites range in size from a few millimetres to more than **60 centimetres –** as long as a child's arm! #0212

A scientist who studies dinosaur poo is called a palaeoscatologist. #0213

55

LITTLE AND LARGE FACTFILE

ARGENTINOSAURUS

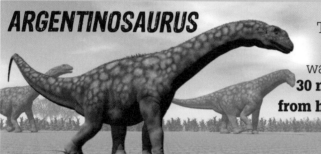

This gigantic plant eater was more than **30 metres long from head to tail.**

#0214

A SINGLE **ARGENTINOSAURUS** SPINAL COLUMN VERTEBRA WAS OVER **1.2 METRES THICK!**

#0215

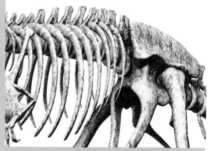

Argentinosaurus is the **longest** dinosaur ever found and, at up to **100 TONNES,** was the **HEAVIEST LAND ANIMAL EVER.**

#0216

A 60-TONNE, 26-METRE *Dreadnoughtus* specimen discovered in Argentina was a youngster, so still had **MORE GROWING TO DO.**

#0217

DREADNOUGHTUS was **TEN TIMES HEAVIER** than *Tyrannosaurus rex.*

X 10

#0218

SPINOSAURUS

may be the **biggest meat-eating dinosaur,** possibly even **larger** than *Tyrannosaurus rex* and *Giganotosaurus.*

#0219

Giraffatitan was **23 metres long** and was the **largest** animal to walk the Earth.

#0220

LEAELLYNASAURA'S TAIL WAS **THREE TIMES** LONGER THAN ITS BODY. #0221

AT LESS THAN **1 METRE TALL,** the little plant eater **Lesothosaurus** was the size of a **BIG TURKEY** and weighed only 4 to 7 kilograms. #0223

The **longest** DINOSAUR HORNS, at more than **1 METRE LONG,** were probably those belonging to **COAHUILACERATOPS.** #0225

Brachiosaurus weighed up to **80 TONNES...** ...that's as much as 17 **AFRICAN ELEPHANTS.** #0222

Brachiosaurus was about **15 metres tall,** but the massive *Sauroposeidon* was possibly **even taller at 18 metres.** #0224

THE SMALLEST **DINOSAUR EGGS** FOUND SO FAR WERE LAID BY *MUSSAURUS* AND WERE ONLY **2.5 CENTIMETRES LONG.** #0226

THE **BIGGEST DINOSAUR EGGS** were probably laid by **Hypselosaurus** or **Gargantuavis** – each egg was **AS BIG AS A BASKETBALL.** #0227

DINOSAUR
HABITATS

CHAPTER 3

Dinosaurs are

SUPER SURVIVORS!

For over almost **165 MILLION** years, dinosaurs and other prehistoric creatures adapted to climate changes and lived **EVERYWHERE...**

...from deserts to forests and from swamps to mountains.

#0228

6 FACTS ABOUT DESERT DINOSAURS

Many Triassic dinosaurs lived in dry, harsh landscapes alongside **lizards** and **early mammals.**

#0229

LARGE bodies helped desert dinosaurs keep cool — just like today's **ELEPHANTS!**

#0230

Fossils of **PROTOCERATOPS** and **VELOCIRAPTOR in mortal combat** were preserved by a fierce desert sandstorm 80 million years ago.

#0231

PLATEOSAURUS lived in dry areas with scrubby plant growth. It may have had to travel long distances to find food.

#0232

GIGANTORAPTOR

had splayed toes to
help it walk on soft
sand without sinking. #0233

When the blazing
SUN became too hot,
ANKYLOSAURUS may
have dug out a nice
cool pit in which to rest.
#0234

FACTS ABOUT
8 ROAMING THE PLAINS

For most of the **Mesozoic Era,** plant-eating dinosaurs ate the leaves of low-growing plants, shrubs and trees on **wide-open areas of land** known as **plains.** #0235

Hundreds of thousands of plant-eating dinosaurs, such as *LAMBEOSAURUS,* roamed the plains in herds.

#0236

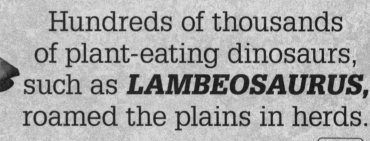

Each year, herds of *CAMARASAURUS* migrated more than **300 kilometres** across the plains to the mountains, looking for food. #0237

With nowhere to hide, **CERATOPSIAN DINOSAURS,** such as *Triceratops,* had to keep a constant watch for predatory theropods. #0238

Some horn-faced ceratopsians, such as **PROTOCERATOPS** and **ZUNICERATOPS**, roamed across the vast, dusty, windswept plains. #0239

Plants, such as ferns, grew on the plains and provided food for **RHINOREX** and **LATIRHINUS,** the duck-billed hadrosaurs that grazed there. #0240

Scientists know that *TYRANNOSAURUS REX* hunted dinosaurs that lived on the plains because the digested remains of a *Triceratops* have been found in its **FOSSILIZED POO.** #0241

HUGE SAUROPODS, SUCH AS **ARGENTINOSAURUS,** LIVED ON THE PLAINS. #0242

9 FACTS ABOUT LIFE IN THE MOUNTAINS

On **steep mountain slopes,** rain washed away the soil, making it almost impossible for fossils to form.

#0243

During the **MESOZOIC ERA, new mountains** formed as **Earth's crust pushed up** over a **long** period of time. #0244

A **200-MILLION-YEAR-OLD** *Diplodocus*-like dinosaur, named *Glacialisaurus*, was found on Mount Kirkpatrick, Antarctica.

#0245

Scientists do **not know** if dinosaurs lived in mountainous areas because **few fossils** have been found there.

#0246

Armoured dinosaurs, such as **EDMONTONIA,** may have lived high in the mountains, but when they died their bones were **washed down** to lower areas.

#0247

During the late Jurassic period, 140 million years ago, the **SEVIER MOUNTAINS** formed in what is now North America.

#0248

In 2008, fossil bones of a dinosaur called **SUSTUT** were found in British Columbia, Canada. *Sustut* was the first dinosaur to be discovered in the **Canadian mountains** and may even be a **new species!**

#0249

New mountain ranges shaped the evolution of dinosaurs, cutting off dinosaurs from the rest of the land so that they evolved into new species.

#0250

Dinosaur fossils found in the remote Antarctic mountains could belong to a new species, possibly related to *Heterodontosaurus*.

#0251

FACTS ABOUT
6 FOREST DINOSAURS

When dinosaurs roamed **ANTARCTICA,** 160 million years ago it was warmer and had **forests!**

#0252

Forest-dwelling **ARCHAEOPTERYX** flew above the trees and lakes of what is now **WESTERN EUROPE,** and stalked small prey that lived along the riverbanks.

#0253

Prehistoric conifers had **tough needles** that helped them survive cool climates and protected them from most of the hungry, tree-eating dinosaurs, such as *DRYOSAURUS.*

#0254

BRACHIOSAURUS

used its 8-metre-long neck to feed on leaves found on the highest treetops. #0255

In Asian forests, **MAMENCHISAURUS** dinosaurs travelled in herds, their long necks parallel to the ground, probing between the forest trees to find foliage, horsetails and ferns.

#0256

Brachiosaurus munched its way through **immense conifer forests,** enjoying even the tough-needled monkey-puzzles and cypresses.

#0257

7 FACTS ABOUT RIVERSIDE DWELLING

GALLIMIMUS may have eaten insects, grubs and plants by sieving river mud with the comb-like plates in its mouth.

#0258

Dinosaurs didn't live in rivers; they prowled around the edges. Some, such as **SPINOSAURUS,** may have been very good at catching fish.

#0259

GALLIMIMUS ran at almost **70 kilometres per hour** along the riverbank mud. #0260

We know that packs of **COELOPHYSIS** lived by rivers because **fossil footprints** have been found in what is now the United States.

#0261

68

Rivers flowed down from the uplands to bring life-giving water into desert areas for dinosaurs such as **PLATEOSAURUS** and **LILIENSTERNUS.**

#0262

River **MOSASAURS** were **dangerous, meat-eating reptiles** that fed on small crocodiles, turtles and other fish.

#0263

River-dwelling **MOSASAURS** grew up to **6 METRES** in length.

#0264

69

10 FACTS ABOUT WETLAND DINOSAURS

Swampy, wetland areas were home to many dinosaurs, including **POLACANTHUS** and the small **HYPSILOPHODON**.

#0265

In the early Cretaceous, low-lying plains became **flooded** with water and sediments from hilly areas to create **wetlands**. #0266

WETLANDS ARE **SOGGY, BOGGY** LANDS THAT COVERED MUCH OF THE AREA THAT IS NOW EUROPE DURING THE CRETACEOUS.

#0267

At more than **10 METRES LONG,** wetland dinosaur *IGUANODON* was bigger than an **elephant!**

#0268

Wetland sauropods, including **BRACHIOSAURUS,** fed on the horsetails and ferns that grew at the edges of the swamps.

#0269

Spiny *POLACANTHUS* was a squat, four-legged, plant-eating dinosaur that grazed on low-growing, wetland plants.

#0270

HYPSILOPHODON was a small, plant-eating dinosaur. It held its body horizontally and **ran fast** on its hind legs along the swampy shores. #0271

In China, 125 million years ago, the **Cretaceous swamp** was home to a dinosaur called **Dilong,** whose name means 'Emperor Dragon'. #0272

TWO-LEGGED *DILONG* LIVED IN THE SWAMPY LAND THAT IS NOW IN EASTERN ASIA. IT WAS THE FIRST TYRANNOSAUROID TO BE DISCOVERED WITH **FEATHERS.** #0273

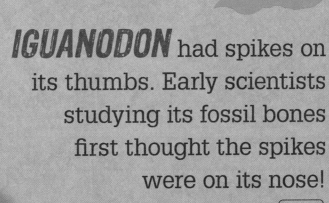

IGUANODON had spikes on its thumbs. Early scientists studying its fossil bones first thought the spikes were on its nose! #0274

71

6 FACTS ABOUT SWAMP FORESTS

The late **CRETACEOUS** swamp forests were full of plants, including the first flowers. #0275

Flowers may have been a vital food for **HUGE** herds of duck-billed

HADROSAURS.

#0276

HADROSAURS used their mouths to clip off forest vegetation, and their **many tiny teeth** to grind it down. #0277

72

Agile theropods such as
TYRANNOSAURUS REX
may have lurked among
the trees to ambush
duck-billed dinosaurs
and other plant eaters
of the swamp forest.

#0278

TROODON
probably ate other
dinosaurs' eggs, small
mammals, lizards and
invertebrates that lived
in the Cretaceous
swamp forests.

#0279

PARASAUROLOPHUS

had a head crest packed with hollow tubes, which
probably helped it to signal by **trumpeting** to others
in the herd as they moved through the forest.

#0280

73

7 FACTS ABOUT
SHALLOW SEAS AND LAGOONS

During the **JURASSIC** and **CRETACEOUS,** shallow seas and great lagoons drew many dinosaurs to the water's edge. #0281

Lagoons were separated from the sea by reefs and were ideal **fossil-forming** zones. #0282

NOTHOSAURUS was an early sea reptile with interlocking teeth that **SNAPPED** together to catch unsuspecting dinosaurs that came too close to the water's edge. #0283

When dinosaurs died in the water, they **sank** straight to the bottom and became **preserved** in the soft silt. #0284

74

Pterosaur fossils, including **PTERODACTYLUS, RHAMPHORHYNCHUS** and **ANUROGNATHUS,** were discovered in what was a salty lagoon in Solnhofen, Germany. #0285

ARCHAEOPTERYX and **COMPSOGNATHUS** lived on the shores of a lagoon in Solnhofen, Germany, around 150 million years ago. #0286

NOTHOSAURUS came ashore to lay eggs but, if frightened, went straight back to the safety of the lagoon. #0287

7 FACTS ABOUT SEASHORE HABITATS

When **coastal dinosaurs** died, their remains were washed into the sea, which helped to preserve them.

#0288

ROAMING along the coastline **millions of years ago** were...

...meat-eating **theropods**,

...plant-eating dinosaurs

...and early beaked dinosaurs.

#0289

ANKYLOSAURUS was one of the heavily armoured dinosaurs that ambled along estuaries and coastlines 67 million years ago.

#0290

HUNGAROSAURUS was a heavily armoured dinosaur that probably lived near the seashore. #0291

HUNGAROSAURUS

fossils have been found next to those of **fish, crocodiles** and **turtles.** #0292

PLANICOXA

was a four-legged dinosaur that could rear up on its hind legs to reach leaves from shoreline trees. #0293

The remains of around **300,000 dinosaur eggs** were found at an ancient **seashore nesting site** in what is now north-eastern Spain. #0294

8 FACTS ABOUT OCEAN LIVING

Giant **ICHTHYOSAURS**, sea reptiles that looked like modern-day fish, ruled the oceans in the early Triassic, **240 million** years ago. #0295

Late in the Triassic, **205 million** years ago, the first **PLESIOSAURS** swam the ocean. #0296

Cymbospondylus was a sleek, powerful predator that grew up to **10 metres in length**. It was the **largest** ichthyosaur ever to have evolved. #0297

Liopleurodon, a pliosaur, was one of the largest ocean predators **of its time.** Scientists know from its **huge** nostrils that it had an extremely good sense of smell and would have been a **highly efficient predator.** #0298

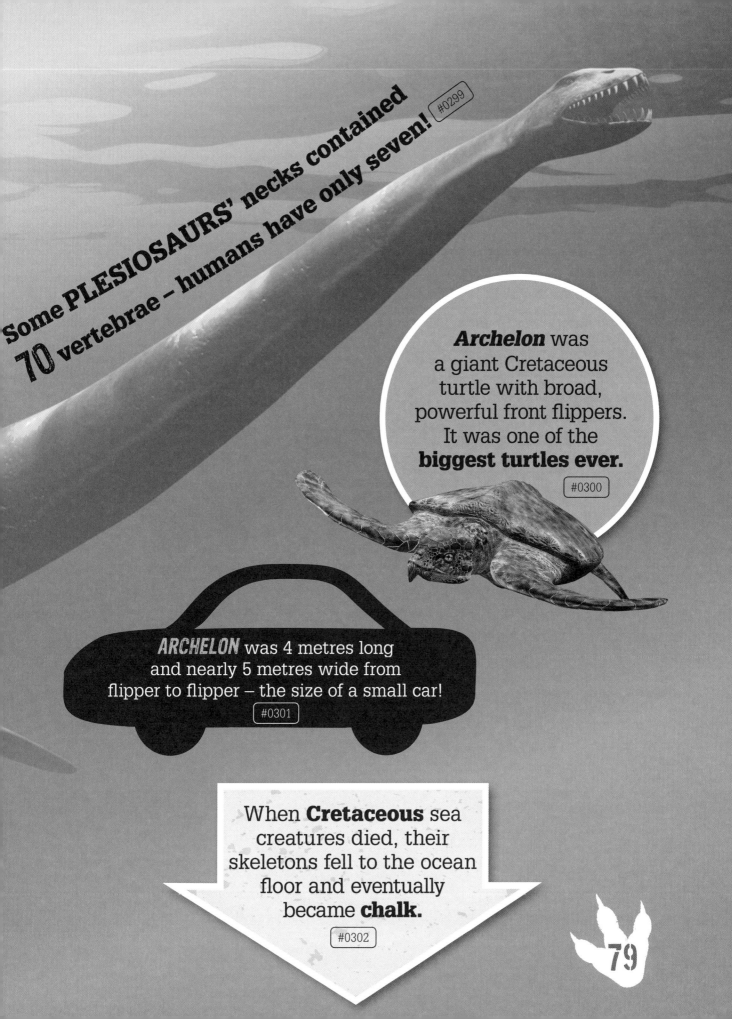

Some **PLESIOSAURS'** necks contained 70 vertebrae – humans have only seven! #0299

Archelon was a giant Cretaceous turtle with broad, powerful front flippers. It was one of the **biggest turtles ever.** #0300

ARCHELON was 4 metres long and nearly 5 metres wide from flipper to flipper – the size of a small car! #0301

When **Cretaceous** sea creatures died, their skeletons fell to the ocean floor and eventually became **chalk.** #0302

79

8 FACTS ABOUT
ISLAND LIFE

After Earth's
supercontinent, Pangaea,
split up, the world's oceans,
seas and lakes became
dotted with tiny islands.

#0303

**DINOSAURS that lived on
islands gradually evolved into
much smaller 'DWARF SPECIES'
because of a lack of food.**

#0304

PTEROSAURS
lived in coastal areas
and some would have
soared over the islands,
swooping down to catch
fish from the sea.

#0305

A small island
could only support
a small population
of dinosaurs.

#0306

TELMATOSAURUS,
a hadrosaur dinosaur, became
a dwarf species on Hateg
Island, which later became
part of **Romania.**

#0307

Dinosaurs on islands had few large **predators.**

#0308

MAGYAROSAURUS
was a relative of the giant
ARGENTINOSAURUS,
but because it lived on an island,
it never grew larger
than a horse. #0309

Three-metre-long
STRUTHIOSAURUS
was an island-dwelling
'DWARF DINOSAUR' that fed
on shoreline plants. #0310

81

7 FACTS ABOUT POLAR DINOSAURS

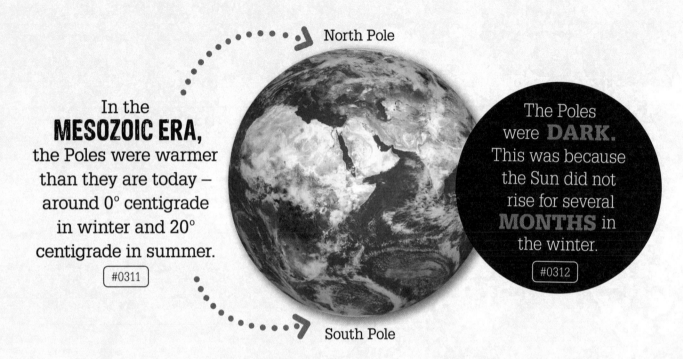

North Pole

South Pole

In the **MESOZOIC ERA,** the Poles were warmer than they are today – around 0° centigrade in winter and 20° centigrade in summer.
#0311

The Poles were **DARK.** This was because the Sun did not rise for several **MONTHS** in the winter.
#0312

LEAELLYNASAURA had big eyes to see in the Polar darkness and dug burrows to keep warm. #0313

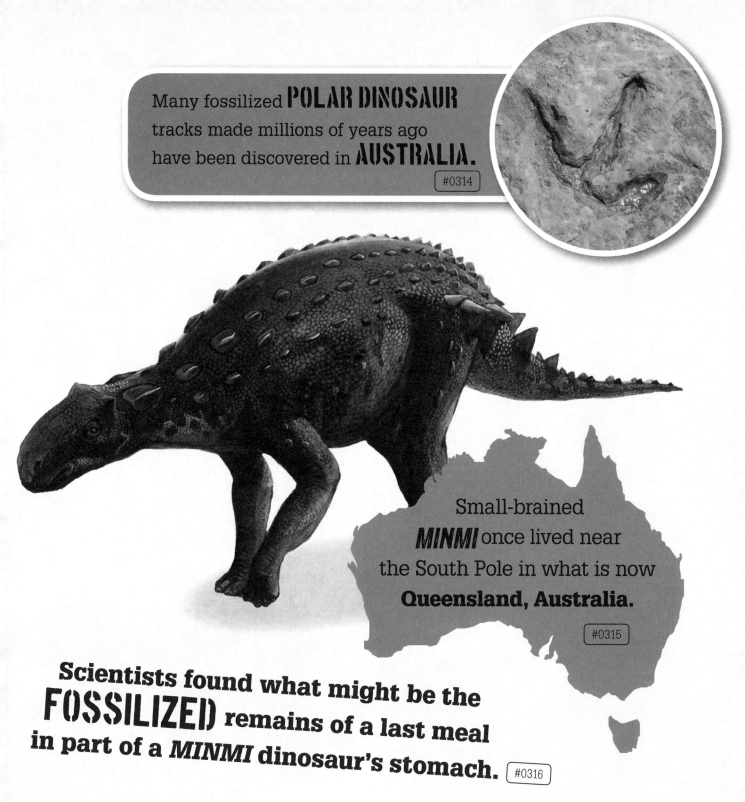

Many fossilized **POLAR DINOSAUR** tracks made millions of years ago have been discovered in **AUSTRALIA.**

#0314

Small-brained **MINMI** once lived near the South Pole in what is now **Queensland, Australia.**

#0315

Scientists found what might be the **FOSSILIZED** remains of a last meal in part of a **MINMI** dinosaur's stomach.

#0316

MINMI'S fossilized stomach contents included what may have been **twigs** or **stems,** bundles of **leaf tissues** and **seeds.** This tells us about the plants it fed on near the South Pole!

#0317

83

8 FACTS ABOUT DINOSAURS AND VOLCANOES

There were many more **VOLCANOES** during the Mesozoic Era than there are today.

#0318

When a volcano **ERUPTED,** poisonous gas and fine hot ash rained down, **KILLING** dinosaurs, other animals and plants.

#0319

Volcanic eruptions killed **MANY** dinosaurs, but the ash preserved their **nests, eggs, bones** and **footprints.**

#0320

Vast layers of ancient volcanic ash in **China** preserved fossils of dinosaurs, such as **SHUVUUIA,** for millions of years.

#0321

84

Scientists can work out the age of ANCIENT ASH and from this they can estimate how long ago dinosaurs lived.

#0322

Fossil bones from dinosaurs killed by volcanic eruptions contain fine **spiderweb cracks,** just like those of the human victims in Pompeii, Italy, when Mount Vesuvius

EXPLODED! #0323

Dinosaurs killed by one eruption in **China** died with their limbs stretched out.

#0324

Scientists **analysed** rock in China's Liaoning Province and found around **24** fossilized young dinosaur skeletons. They found that the dinosaurs were probably caught in one **HUGE VOLCANIC EXPLOSION** of water, mud and rock.

#0325

DINOSAUR HABITAT
FACTFILE

A **desert sandstorm** could **KILL** a dinosaur, burying it in **tonnes** of sand.

#0326

Just like today, prehistoric deserts had **OASES** where dinosaurs would gather.

#0327

DINOSAURS NEEDED TO DRINK FROM LIFE-SAVING OASES, BUT SOMETIMES GOT **SUCKED** INTO DEADLY **QUICKSAND.**

#0328

Water trapped behind **reefs** formed warm, shallow **LAGOONS,** but as the water evaporated, the salt grew ever more **dense** and became **TOXIC** to dinosaurs.

#0330

The bottoms of **LAGOONS** were poisonous, with little oxygen and lots of minerals. Prehistoric creatures that ended up in these murky depths did not last long.

#0331

SWARMS OF **INSECTS** LIVED NEAR THE LAKES WHERE THE REPTILES, **GREAT** AND small, SWAM AND HUNTED.

#0329

Many **pterosaurs** lived on islands scattered in lagoons.

#0332

The **CRETACEOUS PLAINS** were similar to the African plains today. Instead of zebras, great herds of dinosaurs **roamed the land with predators close behind.** #0333

Long-necked sauropods were the major plant eaters right through the **Jurassic.** #0334

Sauropods travelled through forests of **CONIFERS, GINKGOES** and **TREE FERNS,** tramping from one thicket to another in **search of food.** #0335

Utah's Dinosaur National Monument was once a **riverbank forest** and home to many dinosaurs. #0336

Fossil bones of many **CENTROSAURUS** dinosaurs were found in **ALBERTA, CANADA.**

They may have been killed by a **HUGE** storm that flooded the coastal landscape. #0337

TAR PITS

WERE DEADLY. AS ONE ANIMAL FELL IN, OTHERS TRIED TO EAT IT AND WERE SOON ALSO TRAPPED. #0339

Lakes that formed in **DEEP RIFT VALLEYS** provided fresh water that supported a **GREAT** variety of life, such as mammals, fish, insects and dinosaurs. #0341

FOSSILIZED DINOSAUR TRACKS reveal that dinosaurs migrated for **hundreds of kilometres** along beaches. #0338

As dinosaurs evolved, so did the **plants** they ate. Plants survived by their ability to scatter seeds that could grow even when the parent plant had been **swallowed up!** #0340

DINOSAUR DIETS

Finding something to eat and not being **EATEN** took up most of the day for any plant-eating dinosaur. #0342

CHAPTER 4

9 FACTS ABOUT PLANT EATERS

Scientists look at the fossilized teeth of each type of plant-eating dinosaur to find out whether it ate soft or tough plant material. #0343

The **LENGTH** of a plant eater's neck helps reveal what type of leaves it ate...

...the **LONGER** its neck, the **HIGHER** it could reach! #0344

Many peaceful plant eaters had spikes, horns and bumps that looked **FEROCIOUS.** #0345

MAMENCHISAURUS used its 11-metre neck to reach its food! #0346

STYRACOSAURUS had a head frill like an enormous collar. This helped to **protect** its **neck** from attacking meat eaters. #0347

When **STEGOSAURUS** was nervous or angry, its backplates may have filled with blood, making them turn crimson. #0348

BARAPASAURUS, like other **sauropods,** had a **fermentation chamber** in its gut! #0349

A **fermentation chamber** helped dinosaurs to **process** tough plants. It contained **bacteria** that broke down plant material, making it easier to **digest.** #0350

Plant-eating sauropod dinosaurs probably produced lots of **GAS!** #0351

91

13 FACTS ABOUT DEADLY MEAT EATERS

Meat-eating dinosaurs included the **RUTHLESS RAPTORS**, which had muscular jaws and grasping clawed hands. #0352

Some raptors were as **small** as chickens; others were **taller** than a human being! #0353

UTAHRAPTOR could probably smell prey from at least **1.5** kilometres away. #0354

TYRANNOSAURUS REX teeth could rip off up to **230** kilograms of flesh in a **single bite!** #035

The tiny dinosaur **PARVICURSOR** fed on **termites.** #0356

NEOVENATOR was a meat-eating dinosuar that **tore chunks** out of its prey. #0357

SKORPIOVENATOR

may have arched its head back then swung it down, driving its teeth into its prey's flesh. #0358

MAJUNGASAURUS had a broad, short snout, perfect for biting and holding its prey. #0359

MAJUNGASAURUS ate sauropods – and each other! #0360

STOMATOSUCHUS was a **10-metre-long** crocodilian that lived alongside the dinosaurs. #0361

STOMATOSUCHUS competed with meat-eating dinosaurs, gulping small creatures into its pelican-like pouch. #0362

Insects, lizards and **turtles** were all food for dinosaurs. #0363

Dinosaurs often searched for meals that didn't fight back, such as **EGGS.** #0364

93

FACTS ABOUT
7 DINOSAUR ATTACKS

An attacking dinosaur may have **bitten, slashed** or **knocked** down and **trampled** its prey. #0365

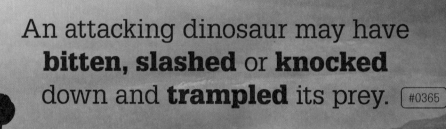

Two **Ankylosaurus** may have used their **tail clubs** in fights over territory or mates. #0366

VELOCIRAPTOR was **FAST** and **AGILE**. It could leap in the air and slash its prey using its sharp claws. #0367

To ward off ferocious meat eaters, long-tailed sauropods, such as *Diplodocus*, may have **whipped** them with their long tails.

#0368

Attacking dinosaurs would single out the **young** or **weak** in a herd.

#0369

GIGANOTOSAURUS

was one of the largest meat-eating dinosaurs to ever thunder across the land.

#0370

One **GIGANOTOSAURUS** would have been terrifying, but these savage giants may have **hunted in packs.**

#0371

FACTS ABOUT
8 GRAZING DINOSAURS

The Jurassic landscape was full of dinosaurs that ate **mosses, ferns, horsetails, cycads, ginkgoes** and **conifers.** #0372

Flowering plants first appeared 125 million years ago, which meant that late Cretaceous dinosaurs could have eaten **fruit.** #0373

The mouths of some plant eaters, such as *PLATEOSAURUS*, were packed with **leaf-shaped** teeth. Other plant eaters, such as *DIPLODOCUS*, had teeth that were long and thin and looked more like pencils. #0374

BLUNT TEETH
were great for **stripping** vegetation such as twigs and leaves. #0375

FLAT TEETH
could help to **grind** up tough plant fibres. #0376

96

Ankylosaurs had teeth designed for slicing plants, but not for chewing their food. #0377

Plant-eating **ORNITHOMIMUS**' name means **"bird mimic"** because it looks similar to a modern-day **OSTRICH** or **EMU**. #0378

ORNITHOMIMUS mainly ate plants, but also occasionally fed on **small animals**. #0379

12 FACTS ABOUT HOW NOT TO BE EATEN!

#0380

Many modern-day plant eaters try to **blend** into the background, so some dinosaurs probably had **SPOTS** or **STRIPES**.
#0380

Fossilized skin is extremely rare and never keeps its colour, so scientists cannot tell for sure if dinosaurs were **CAMOUFLAGED** or not. #0381

Dinosaurs did **NOT** want to be flipped over: soft bellies were **vulnerable.** Being heavy with sturdy legs helped to avoid this.
#0382

TRICERATOPS three enormous horns and its almost 1-metre-wide frill helped defend it against attacks. #0383

If threatened, a group of **PROTOCERATOPS** stood in a circle around their babies or eggs to protect them. #0384

Thick skin gave **PINACOSAURUS** very useful protection. #0385

TALARURUS had thorny spikes on its back to ward off would-be attackers. #0386

98

STEGOCERAS' head was **40 times thicker** than a human skull. #0387

Head frills and spikes helped to protect **CHASMOSAURUS'** neck. #0388

Tough, **leathery skin** protected the dinosaurs from predators' bites... #0389

...while **sharp horns** were able to pierce the thick skin of predators such as *Tyrannosaurus rex*. #0390

For some dinosaurs, the best strategy was to run away – **FAST!** #0391

9 FACTS ABOUT
GASTROLITHS

Plant-eating dinosaurs **swallowed rocks** to help them digest their food. These rocks were called **GASTROLITHS.** #0392

Gastroliths helped to **GRIND UP** plant fibres inside the dinosaur. #0393

OMEISAURUS ate so much each day that it didn't have time to chew its food. Instead, it swallowed plants whole and gastroliths did the work! #0394

A fossil gastrolith from a dinosaur can weigh several kilograms. #0395

100

Some gastroliths found near sauropod skeletons are about **10 CENTIMETRES** long. #0396

Gastroliths probably **ROLLED** and **TUMBLED** in the digestive tract, sinking low down and grinding the food like a mill.

#0397

PLESIOSAURS may have swallowed **gastroliths** to counteract buoyancy and help them stay down in the water.

#0398

Minerals in gastroliths may have been a **USEFUL DIET SUPPLEMENT.**

#0399

Modern-day **animals,** such as **crocodiles, alligators, seals** and **sea lions,** swallow gastroliths.

#0400

11 FACTS ABOUT THE DINOSAUR FOOD CHAIN

There were **three layers** in the dinosaur food chain: **primary** producers, **primary** consumers and **secondary** consumers.
#0401

The **dinosaur food chain** started with plants and ended with MEAT EATERS.
#0402

Plants were primary producers. They thrived if there was **plenty of rain and sunshine.**
#0403

PLANT EATERS
were the primary consumers. They grew **plump** by eating lots of plants. This, in turn, made them **good to eat.**
#0404

Meat eaters, such as TYRANNOSAURUS REX and Utahraptor, were secondary consumers. They ate any plant-eating dinosaurs they could catch.
#0405

DINOSAUR DROPPINGS
helped fertilize the soil so **plants grew.** This made more food for plant-eating dinosaurs in the dinosaur food chain.
#0406

If there were **too many meat-eating dinosaurs**, and they ate **too many plant-eating dinosaurs**, it became harder for the meat-eating dinosaurs to

FIND ENOUGH PREY.

#0407

Dinosaur life was a balancing act. A group of large herbivores grazing and munching needed hundreds of hectares of plants to survive and

G-R-O-W.

#0408

If plant food became scarce,

PLANT-EATING DINOSAURS

starved and died.

#0409

If plant-eating dinosaur numbers **dropped, MEAT-EATING** dinosaurs **DIED** and their numbers dropped, too.

#0410

Dinosaur eggs were part of a food chain. Early mammals and

LIZARDS FEASTED ON THEM!

#0411

103

DINOSAUR DIET
FACTFILE

To find out what **dinosaurs ate,** researchers **STUDY THEIR SKULLS,** **teeth and jaws,** fossilized **stomach contents** and **DINOSAUR POO.** #0412

BARYONYX had **96 TEETH,** many more than its fellow theropod, *Tyrannosaurus rex,* which had only **60 TEETH.** #0414

Baryonyx's jaws were **ANGLED** to keep its **FISHY** meal from wriggling out. #0415

BARYONYX hooked fish out of the water

with its **clawed thumb.** #0413

The name **OVIRAPTOR** means **"EGG HUNTER".** #0416

When the first **OVIRAPTOR** was discovered, it was surrounded by lots of eggs. Scientists later realized it wasn't **eating** the eggs, but **protecting** its young! #0417

OVIRAPTOR had no teeth but a bird-like beak and **REALLY POWERFUL JAWS** so it could crush...

...NUTS,

...SHELLFISH

...AND INSECTS. #0418

OMNIVORES WERE
UNFUSSY
AND ATE BOTH
MEAT AND **PLANTS!**

#0419

Recent discoveries suggest that
SPINOSAURUS may have
waded through water to
hunt for **fish.**   #0420

About
65 PER CENT
of dinosaurs ate
only plants

35 PER CENT
were meat eaters or
ominvores.   #0421

TYRANNOSAURUS
REX
ate meat and so did the
great majority of its
closest relatives, such
as *oviraptor* and the
dromaeosaurs.   #0422

Among the smallest meat
eaters was cat-sized
HESPERONYCHUS
at only
60 TO 80
centimetres long.

#0423

HESPERONYCHUS
probably ate…

...INSECTS,

...SMALL
MAMMALS,

...LIZARDS

...AND BABY
DINOSAURS.

#0425

Tiny **COELUROSAURS**
probably ate tiny **lizards.**

#0424

DINOSAUR
BEHAVIOUR

Scientists study **living birds** to give them an amazing **INSIGHT** into the lives of the dinosaurs, millions of years ago. #0426

CHAPTER 5

10 FACTS ABOUT DINOSAUR EGGS

As far as we know, **ALL** dinosaurs laid eggs.

#0427

Big dinosaurs, such as *GIGANTORAPTOR*, laid eggs in small pits, and may have covered them in earth and leaves.

#0428

Small dinosaurs may have sat on eggs to keep them warm, **just like hens do.**

#0429

Big dinosaurs could not have sat on their eggs without **SMASHING them to pieces!**

#0430

Feathered dinosaurs, such as **CITIPATI,** #0431 spread their long, feathered arms over their eggs to make sure they were **snug and warm.**

Up to
40
eggs have been found
in a **SINGLE NEST.**

#0432

Most dinosaur
eggs had
HARD, BRITTLE
shells, similar
to modern-day
birds' eggs.

#0433

Some dinosaurs
simply left their
eggs in the heat
of the sun to
**HATCH ON
THEIR OWN.**

#0434

The **LARGEST**
dinosaur eggs
were as big as
BASKETBALLS.

#0435

Shells from the largest dinosaur eggs
were up to **5** millimetres thick.

#0436

7 FACTS ABOUT DINOSAUR FAMILIES

Dinosaurs laid **LOTS OF EGGS,** so that at least one hatchling would survive to reach adulthood.
#0437

Some **dinosaur families** may have lived together in herds, **nesting together,** caring for their young and KEEPING **A LOOKOUT FOR DANGER.** #0438

Being part of a group offered greater safety. Large herds could **STAMPEDE** and fend off predators when **ATTACKED.**
#0439

Many young **hatchling dinosaurs** had to look after themselves the moment they **popped** out of the egg. #0440

A nest of **15 FOSSILIZED** *Protoceratops* babies was found in Mongolia, which suggests they were **growing up together,** perhaps watched over by a parent.

#0441

MAIASAURA CARED FOR ITS BABIES after they were born for several weeks, possibly even months.

#0442

Tiny baby sauropods were probably safer coping on their own when they hatched from their eggs – **away from their parents'** BIG FEET.

#0443

8 FACTS ABOUT FIGHTS!

Some dinosaurs **fought to protect** their babies and their **eggs.**

#0444

DINOSAURS attacked THEIR PREY
either singly or with others **in a pack.**

#0445

Megaraptor defended itself by **LASHING OUT** with its **sharp claws.**

#0446

Spring may have been a time of **FIERCE BATTLES,** when male dinosaurs fought for the attention of females.

#0447

112

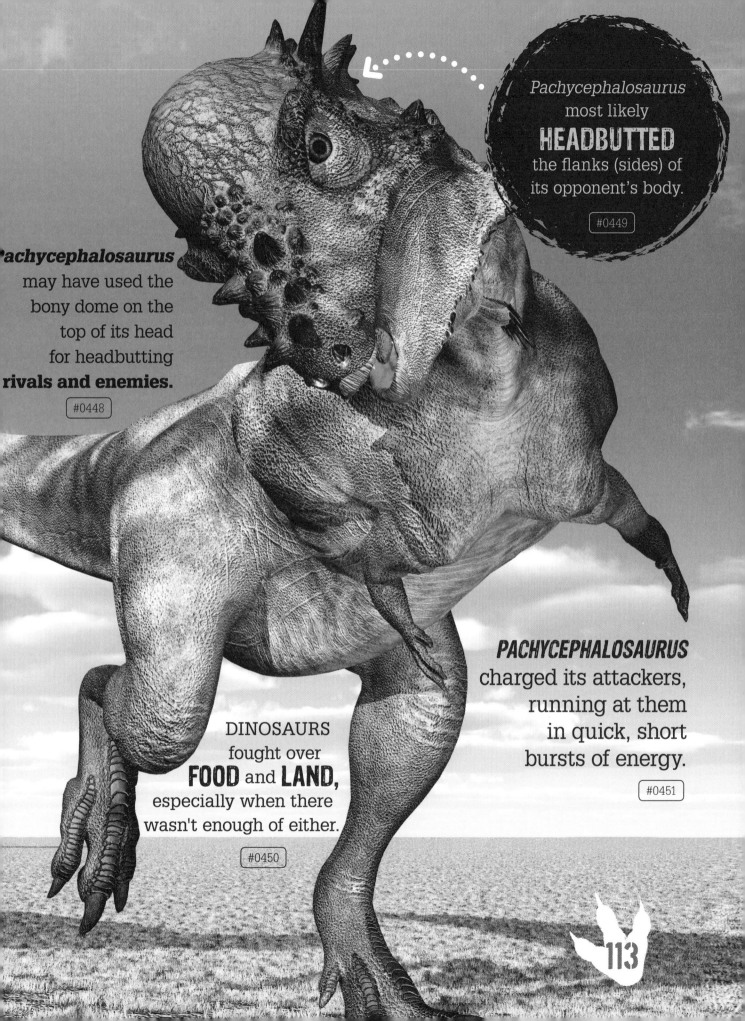

Pachycephalosaurus
most likely
HEADBUTTED
the flanks (sides) of
its opponent's body.

#0449

Pachycephalosaurus
may have used the
bony dome on the
top of its head
for headbutting
rivals and enemies.

#0448

PACHYCEPHALOSAURUS
charged its attackers,
running at them
in quick, short
bursts of energy.

#0451

DINOSAURS
fought over
FOOD and **LAND,**
especially when there
wasn't enough of either.

#0450

8 FACTS ABOUT WINNING DINOSAURS

The animals that were hunted evolved to run **REALLY FAST** to escape, then the hunters evolved to **RUN EVEN FASTER.** #0452

MASSIVE *Tyrannosaurus rex* and other **big meat eaters** were so huge they they could stun a victim by knocking it down to the ground before moving in for the **final kill.** #0453

A duckbill dinosaur fossil was discovered with a healed wound, probably from a *Tyrannosaurus rex.*

This showed it had fought against its attacker and **won!** #0454

Graciliraptor's **small** size and light weight helped it to run from attackers. It was probably one of the **fastest** raptors. #0455

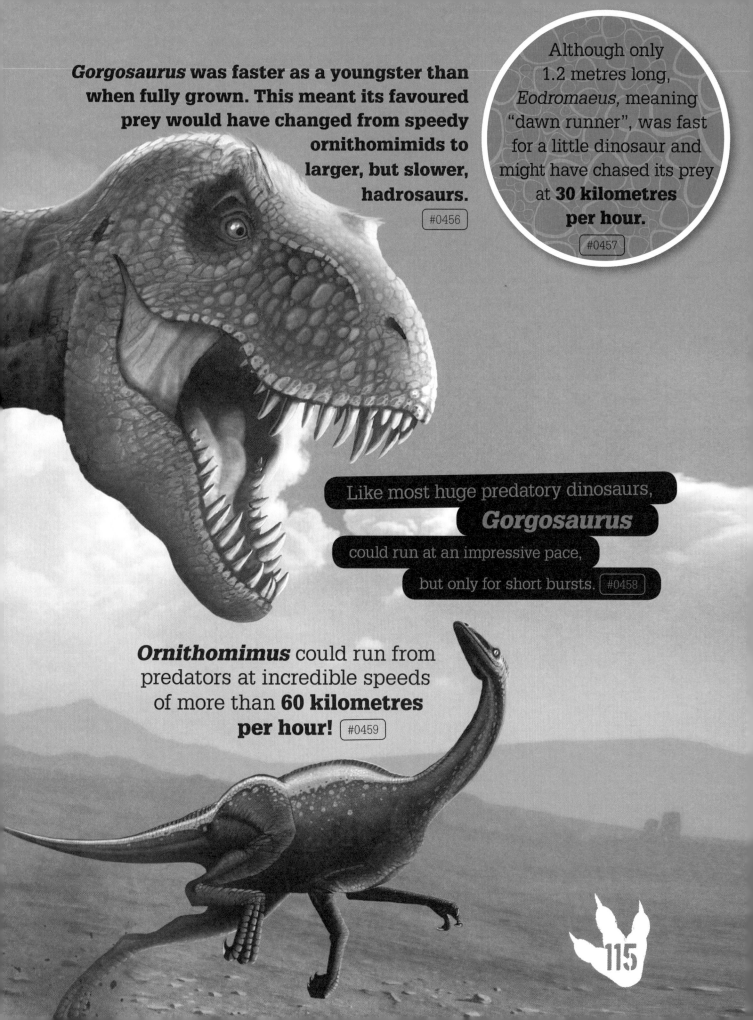

Gorgosaurus was faster as a youngster than when fully grown. This meant its favoured prey would have changed from speedy ornithomimids to larger, but slower, hadrosaurs.

#0456

Although only 1.2 metres long, *Eodromaeus*, meaning "dawn runner", was fast for a little dinosaur and might have chased its prey at **30 kilometres per hour.**

#0457

Like most huge predatory dinosaurs, **Gorgosaurus** could run at an impressive pace, but only for short bursts. #0458

Ornithomimus could run from predators at incredible speeds of more than **60 kilometres per hour!** #0459

9 FACTS ABOUT DINOSAUR COMMUNICATION

Dinosaurs were **NOISY,** but it's been more than 66 million years since they were last heard on Earth! #0460

Scientists believe that dinosaurs communicated using **body movements and sound,** because that's how **modern-day birds** and **reptiles COMMUNICATE.** #0461

Soft tissues, such as **vocal chords,** don't survive as fossils. This makes it difficult to know exactly what noises dinosaurs may have made. #0462

The **WHIP-CRACKING** sound made by a **Barosaurus' tail** would have travelled long distances and may have attracted potential mates. #0463

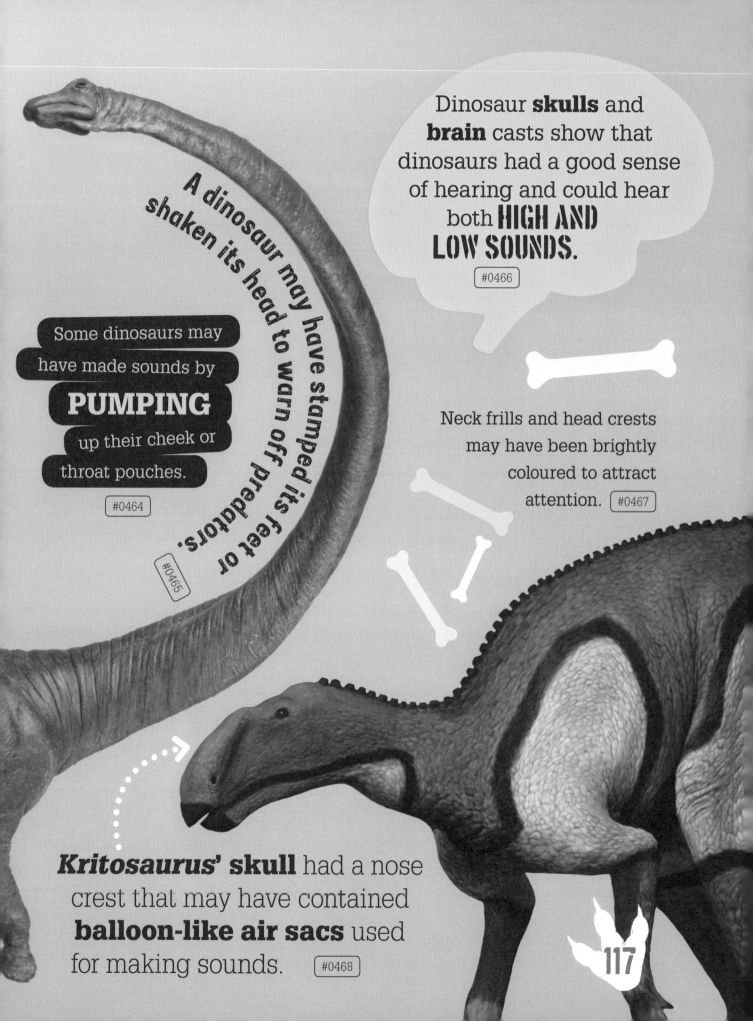

Dinosaur **skulls** and **brain** casts show that dinosaurs had a good sense of hearing and could hear both **HIGH AND LOW SOUNDS.**

#0466

Some dinosaurs may have made sounds by **PUMPING** up their cheek or throat pouches.

#0464

A dinosaur may have stamped its feet or shaken its head to warn off predators.

#0465

Neck frills and head crests may have been brightly coloured to attract attention. #0467

Kritosaurus' **skull** had a nose crest that may have contained **balloon-like air sacs** used for making sounds. #0468

8 FACTS ABOUT
DINOSAURS AT REST

Many dinosaurs had no nest or burrow to rest in – they were constantly on the move.

#0469

A fossilized *Segisaurus* was found in what may have been a resting position, with its legs tucked beneath its body.

#0470

A fossil skeleton of a small, sleeping Chinese dinosaur fossil was named *Mei*, meaning **"sleeping soundly"**.

#0471

Fossils found in China, in 2007, tell us that some dinosaurs tucked themselves up, just like **modern-day birds.**

#0472

DINOSAUR BURROWS

made by *Oryctodromeus* have been found in Montana, United States.

#0473

An ***ORYCTODROMEUS*** burrow reached about **50 CENTIMETRES** underground and was just over **2 metres long.**

#0474

Scientists studied **birds'** sleep patterns as a way of speculating whether dinosaurs slept or not. They think it probable that dinosaurs, like birds, only slept for short spells.

#0475

Feathered dinosaur ***Sinornithosaurus*** was only active for short periods of the day and night in its woodland home.

#0476

119

6 FACTS ABOUT DINOSAURS ON THE MOVE

Gigantic pterosaurs may have flown long distances, perhaps **crossing** the **Atlantic** – which was about **300 KILOMETRES WIDE** in places – and flying over Eurasia.

#0477

Dinosaur footprints on long trackways show that dinosaurs **trekked for many kilometres** through what is now Colorado and New Mexico, in the United States.

#0478

Plant-eating dinosaurs would have trekked along well-worn paths in pursuit of better food supplies, **FOLLOWED BY MEAT EATERS.** #0479

Analysis of **dinosaur teeth** shows changes in their make-up that suggest that sauropods, such as **Camarasaurus,** migrated during **the dry season.** #0480

The great dinosaur track that runs 650 kilometres through North America has been named the...

DINOSAUR FREEWAY. #0481

Scientists think that as **dinosaurs evolved to be** **BIGGER,** **with longer legs,** they travelled further to find food.

#0482

121

11 FACTS ABOUT
LIFE ABOVE THE DINOSAURS

PTEROSAURS were flying reptiles and the first creatures with a backbone to flap their wings and achieve powered flight. #0483

Although pterosaurs had light, hollow bones just like birds, they were only distantly related. #0484

There is no such animal as a **pterodactyl,** although lots of people use this name! There is a type of dinosaur called *Pterodactylus*, which belongs to the group called **pterosaurs.** #0485

Pteranodon had a **BACKWARD-POINTING** skull crest, which may have been used to **attract** a **mate.** #0486

A pterosaur's wing stretched from **its very, very long fourth finger.** #0487

When **pterosaur fossils** were first discovered, it was suggested that pterosaurs might have **glided** like flying squirrels or **swum** like penguins. We now know that they **FLEW.** #0488

FOSSIL DISCOVERIES
tell us that young and old pterosaurs may have lived together in large social groups.
#0489

PTEROSAURS
may have buried their eggs on #0490 shorelines.

Pterosaurs died out at the end of the Triassic. #0491

A PTEROSAUR had a large, leathery membrane stretched tautly between its body and long fourth finger. #0492

The largest Pteranodon had an **IMMENSE WINGSPAN** of up to **7 METRES**, which is as big as a small plane. #0493

123

RECORD BREAKER FACTFILE

NYASASAURUS

MAY BE THE **FIRST** DINOSAUR THAT EVER EXISTED. **It lived around 243 million years ago,** which is 10 to 15 million years before dinosaurs were thought to exist!

#0494

EORAPTOR

HELD THE **OLDEST** DINOSAUR TITLE FROM 1993 TO 1999. THIS DOG-SIZED SPRINTER IS **228 TO 231 MILLION YEARS OLD.**

#0495

DROMICEIOMIMUS

WAS ONE OF THE **FASTEST** DINOSAURS, RUNNING UP TO **70 KILOMETRES** PER HOUR TO ESCAPE **HUNGRY THEROPODS.**

#0496

One of the **smartest** dinosaur hunters included **speedy** *Troodon* with its brilliant vision, fine hearing, acrobatic agility and balance.

#0498

The **oldest** known dinosaur fossil to be found in the United Kingdom is of a **210-million-year-old** *Thecodontosaurus.*

#0497

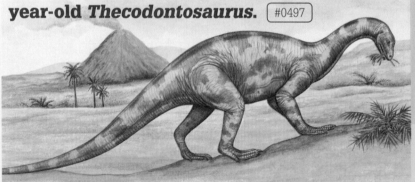

DEINOCHEIRUS had the LONGEST ARMS of any dinosaur – they were 2.5 METRES long!

#0499

The LONGEST dinosaur name is

MICROPACHYCEPHALOSAURUS!

#0500

HUNTING IN THE ARCTIC CIRCLE

was a dinosaur called *Nanuqsaurus*. It may have been the **hardiest** dinosaur and was named after the local word for polar bear, "*nanuq*".

#0501

THE FIRST DINOSAUR REMAINS TO BE DISCOVERED IN THE UNITED STATES were found in 1854. The discovery included teeth from three dinosaurs: **TRACHODON, TROODON AND DEINODON.** #0502

One of the most common fossil dinosaur skeletons found is that of parrot-beaked *Psittacosaurus.*

#0503

THE MOST DINOSAUR SKELETONS EVER TO GO MISSING WERE 18 THAT WERE snatched from Mongolia over a long period of time and returned home by the United States in 2014. #0504

Hundreds of **COELOPHYSIS SKELETONS,** THE **MOST** EVER FOUND TOGETHER, were found in 1947 in **NEW MEXICO, UNITED STATES**. The dinosaurs probably died of thirst at a dried-up water source before being buried in a flash flood. #0505

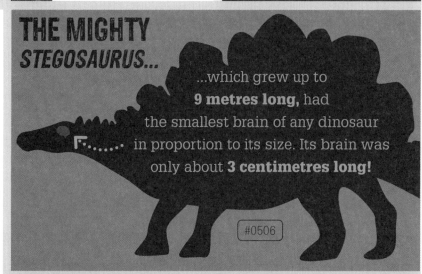

THE MIGHTY STEGOSAURUS... ...which grew up to **9 metres long,** had the smallest brain of any dinosaur in proportion to its size. Its brain was only about **3 centimetres long!** #0506

The **shortest dinosaur name** is now shared by **Mei, Kol** and the recently discovered **Zby.** #0507

The **LARGEST PLIOSAUR** was probably *18 metres long.* #0508

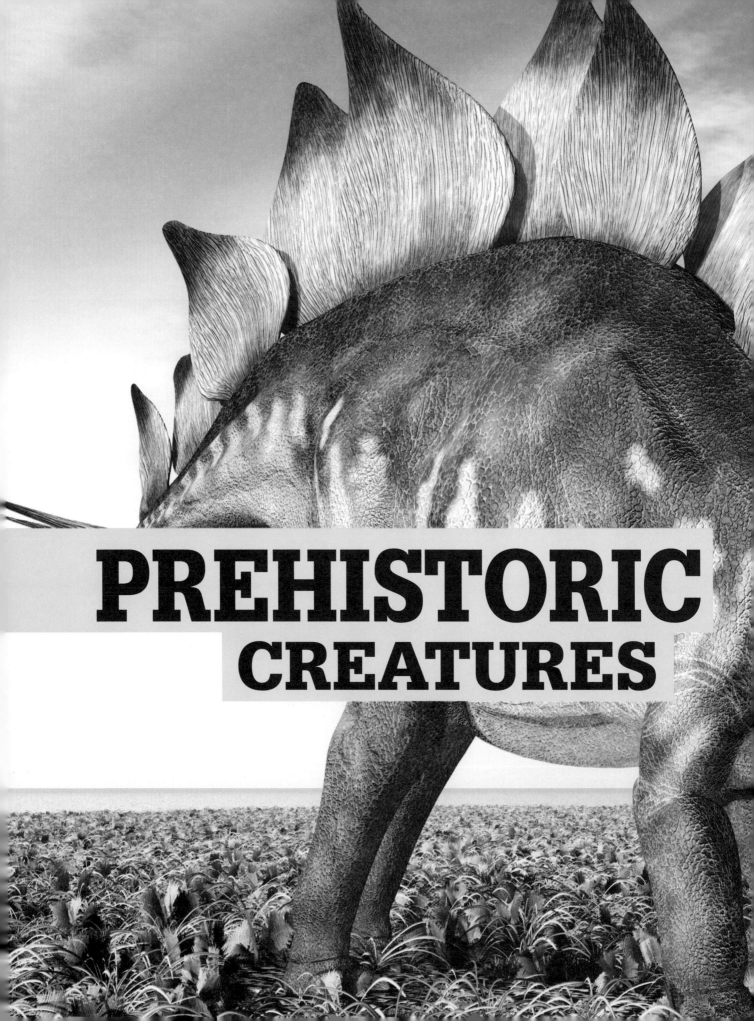

PREHISTORIC
CREATURES

Long ago, *Stegosaurus* munched on plants in subtropical forests...

CHAPTER 6

...ABOUT **150 MILLION YEARS LATER,** **the world's most complete fossilized skeleton,** a *Stegosaurus* from Wyoming, United States, was displayed in London's Natural History Museum.

#0509

Albertaceratops lived

80–75 MILLION YEARS AGO. #0510

A **fossilized skull** belonging to *Albertaceratops* was found in 2001 in Alberta, Canada. #0511

Albertaceratops probably lived in a **large herd,** nibbling away at **small saplings and ferns.** #0512

Albertaceratops **had** FIVE HORNS on its head. #0513

Albertaceratops had unusually **l-o-n-g brow horns.** #0514

Albertaceratops was around **7 metres long.** #0515

128

Albertaceratops worked in groups to **fight** off **predators.** #0516

Albertosaurus lived
70 MILLION YEARS AGO. #0518

Albertosaurus
may have grown to a
LENGTH OF 10 METRES. #0519

An adult Albertosaurus usually measured up to **9 METRES LONG.** #0517

Albertosaurus
was a meat eater with
a **MASSIVE** head.
#0520

Albertosaurus had **two horns** in front of its eyes. #0521

Albertosaurus
had about 60 huge
conical-shaped
SHARP TEETH
in its scissor-
like jaws.
#0522

The first *Albertosaurus* skeleton was found in 1884.
#0523

Albertosaurus
had only **two fingers**
at the end of its
short arms.
#0524

Twenty-six fossil skeletons belonging to *Albertosaurus* were found together. This suggests they **hunted** in **packs.** #0525

7 FACTS ABOUT ALLOSAURUS

Allosaurus roamed across plains, woodlands and wetland shores **150 MILLION YEARS AGO.** #0526

ALLOSAURUS FOSSILS have been found in the **United States** and **Portugal.** #0527

Just like a tiger, meat-eating Allosaurus probably hid, **LYING IN WAIT** for its prey. #0528

Allosaurus could have leaped at least **3 METRES HIGH.** #0529

ALLOSAURUS COULD HAVE RUN AT

30 kilometres per hour.
#0530

Allosaurus' form of attack was to bite and hang on to prey with its **TEETH** and **STRONG JAWS.** #0531

Some *Allosaurus* **skeletons** have **healed broken ribs.** Scientists think that this huge creature would have fallen over if it **RAN TOO FAST.** #0532

9 FACTS ABOUT APATOSAURUS

Apatosaurus lived **147 to 137 million years ago.**

#0533

Apatosaurus lived in what is now **NORTH AMERICA.**

#0534

Apatosaurus was a **harmless giant** and one of the **LARGEST** land animals that has ever existed.

#0535

Apatosaurus used to be called **BRONTOSAURUS.**

#0536

Apatosaurus was **21 to 27 metres long** and **weighed 30 to 35 tonnes.** That's heavier than more than 400 men!

#0537

APATOSAURUS' NOSTRILS WERE ON THE TOP OF ITS HEAD. NO ONE KNOWS WHY! #0538

Fossil bones can get mixed up, and during one reconstruction, scientists put the **WRONG SKULL** on an *Apatosaurus* skeleton body. #0540

APATOSAURUS STOOD so TALL that predators could not reach to attack its head or neck. #0539

Fossilized *Apatosaurus* footprints tell us that tough pads covered its toes, just like those of modern-day elephants. #0541

133

7 FACTS ABOUT ARCHAEOPTERYX

DISCOVERED IN GERMANY IN 1861, *Archaeopteryx* had the **feathers of a bird,** but the **tail, teeth** and **claws** of a **DINOSAUR.** #0542

Archaeopteryx had the coordination, balance and vision needed to fly. #0543

Richard Owen, the creator of London's Natural History Museum, was the first to claim *Archaeopteryx* was a bird. #0545

Archaeopteryx is known as the **FIRST BIRD.** #0544

Archaeopteryx lived **150 million years ago** – previously, no birds were thought to exist that far back in time. #0546

Using a scanner, scientists built a three-dimensional model of *Archaeopteryx's* brain. #0547

Archaeopteryx's brain fitted so tightly into its head that it left an impression behind it on the skull. #0548

Brachiosaurus lived
153 MILLION YEARS AGO.
#0549

Brachiosaurus lived in what is now the **United States.**
#0550

Brachiosaurus was first thought to be one of the largest dinosaurs, but now **EVEN LARGER** dinosaurs, such as *Dreadnoughtus*, have been discovered.
#0551

Brachiosaurus may have been **WARM-BLOODED,** like birds and mammals are today.
#0552

It was **12 to 16 metres tall.**
#0553

In the **MESOZOIC ERA,** meat eaters were less than half the size of *Brachiosaurus*. They probably **chased after easier prey,** leaving *Brachiosaurus* alone to **graze** in **peace.**
#0554

Scientists still do not know whether *Brachiosaurus* held its **LONG NECK** mostly vertically or horizontally, but it could probably **MOVE** between each **POSITION.**
#0555

135

8 FACTS ABOUT COMPSOGNATHUS

Compsognathus lived **150 MILLION YEARS AGO.** #0556

Compsognathus lived in the area that is now **Europe.** #0557

Compsognathus had a long **neck** and **tail...**

Compsognathus was an **AGILE** runner and could run at speeds of up to 63 kilometres per hour. #0559

Compsognathus' body was **no bigger** than a **chicken.**

#0560

...and was about **1 METRE IN LENGTH.**

#0558

Compsognathus **was one of the** first complete fossil skeletons **of any dinosaur to be found.**

#0561

A lizard has been found inside a **fossilized Compsognathus stomach.**

#0562

Compsognathus had a **large brain** for its body size and was probably among the more **intelligent** dinosaurs.

#0563

7 FACTS ABOUT DEINONYCHUS

Deinonychus lived about

115 to 110
MILLION
YEARS AGO.

#0564

Deinonychus lived in the area that is now the **UNITED STATES.**

#0565

Meat-eating hunter *Deinonychus* grew up to

3.4 metres long.

#0566

Deinonychus' tail was stiff, which helped it to balance as it attacked prey.

#0567

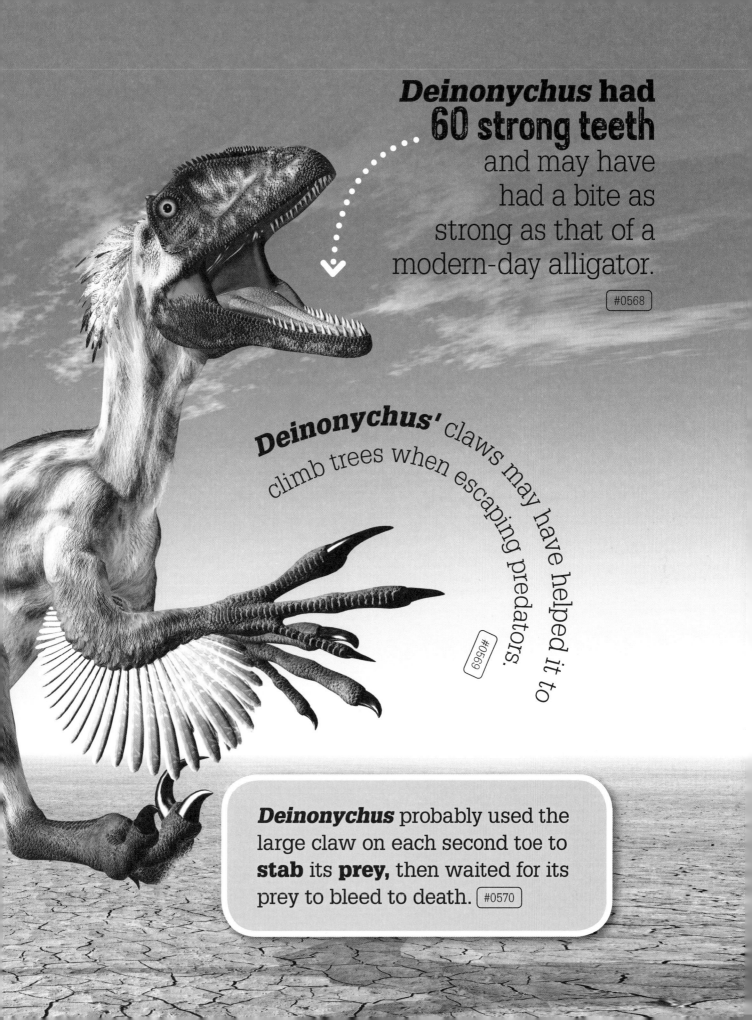

Deinonychus had 60 strong teeth and may have had a bite as strong as that of a modern-day alligator. #0568

Deinonychus' claws may have helped it to climb trees when escaping predators. #0569

Deinonychus probably used the large claw on each second toe to **stab** its **prey,** then waited for its prey to bleed to death. #0570

11 FACTS ABOUT DIPLODOCUS ON DISPLAY

A near-complete **Diplodocus skeleton** was found in the United States in 1898.
#0571

It took **18 months** to make the **replica.**
#0573

When making the *Diplodocus* replica, **missing bones** were cast from bones from four other specimens.
#0574

KING EDWARD VII had a *Diplodocus* replica made for Great Britain.
#0572

King Edward VII's *Diplodocus* replica was completed in 1904. It was shipped to Britain in

36 crates.
#0575

Britain's *Diplodocus* replica was revealed in a special ceremony **on 12th May, 1905.**
#0576

140

The *Diplodocus* replica made for **King Edward VII** was the first **FULL REPLICA SKELETON** of a sauropod dinosaur to go **on display** in the world.
#0577

The *Diplodocus* replica became the **STAR EXHIBIT** in London's Natural History Museum. Its nickname is **DIPPY**. #0578

In total, **10 replica *Diplodocus*** skeletons have been made and sent across the world to different museums. #0579

A *Diplodocus* skeleton had **292 bones.** #0580

The *Diplodocus* replica has been **cleaned** every **two years.** #0581

14 FACTS ABOUT DREADNOUGHTUS

A *Dreadnoughtus* fossil was uncovered in Argentina between 2005 and 2009. #0582

Dreadnoughtus lived AROUND 77 TO 76 MILLION YEARS AGO. #0583

Its **11.2-metre neck** was shaped like a **PIPE!** #0585

Dreadnoughtus is thought to have been the **heaviest** dinosaur ever. #0584

It took **five years** to excavate the colossal *Dreadnoughtus* fossil. #0586

Around **250 bones** from *Dreadnoughtus'* fossil skeleton have been recovered. #0587

Dreadnought[us] was probab[ly] **buried** when th[e] ground turne[d] to **quicksan[d]** during a **floo[d]** #0588

Dreadnoughtus had a house-sized body weighing

nearly 60 tonnes

– as much as a herd of elephants. #0589

The **Dreadnoughtus** specimen that was found was not full-grown so no one knows just how

ENORMOUS

the adults were. #0590

Dreadnoughtus was named after a type of **giant battleship.** #0592

Dreadnoughtus may have been buried so quickly by quicksand that **prowling scavengers** had no chance to **feast on its body.** #0591

Dreadnoughtus had a muscular **8.8-metre-long tail.** #0594

The name *Dreadnoughtus* means **'FEARING NOTHING'.** #0593

Dreadnoughtus' **thigh bone** alone was as **long** as a **man** is **tall.** #0595

143

7 FACTS ABOUT DROMAEOSAURUS

Dromaeosaurus lived **75 MILLION YEARS AGO.** #0596

Dromaeosaurus lived in what is now **North America.** #0597

Dromaeosaurus had **BIG EYES** and looked a little like an emu. #0598

Dromaeosaurus was about **2 METRES** long. #0599

Worn-down teeth suggest that Dromaeosaurus used its jaws for crushing and tearing. #0600

To **kill** its **prey,** Dromaeosaurus relied on its **powerful jaws** rather than its claws. #0601

Dromaeosaurus' bite was **MORE POWERFUL** than Velociraptor's. #0602

Gallimimus lived
70 MILLION YEARS AGO. #0603

One of the biggest chicken-like dinosaurs, *Gallimimus* was **6 METRES** in length. #0604

A **strong tail** gave *Gallimimus* **extra balance** and helped it to turn when **running quickly.** #0605

Some of the bones in a *Gallimimus* jaw were as thin as paper. #0606

The first ***Gallimimus*** fossil remains were found in the Gobi Desert in the early 1970s. #0607

Gallimimus had **HOLLOW BONES** that kept it light. #0608

10 FACTS ABOUT
GIGANOTOSAURUS

Giganotosaurus roamed the Earth

100 TO 97 MILLION YEARS AGO

in swampland in an area that is now
South America. #0609

GIGANOTOSAURUS was a

HUGE MEAT EATER.

#0610

**Weighing
8 to 10 tonnes,**
Giganotosaurus
was as heavy
as a male
**AFRICAN
ELEPHANT.**
#0611

Giganotosaurus
was an incredible
13 METRES LONG!
#0612

Giganotosaurus was so **BIG** and **STRONG**
that it probably could have **killed** some
of the **giant plant eaters.** #0613

Giganotosaurus had a smaller brain than **Tyrannosaurus rex,** but a massive skull.

#0615

Giganotosaurus was **bigger** than Tyrannosaurus rex, but more lightly built.

#0614

One Giganotosaurus specimen was found near to fossils of some huge plant eaters, possibly its prey.

#0616

It had unusually **short arms.**

#0617

Around 70 per cent of a complete **Giganotosaurus skeleton** was found between 1993 and 1994. #0618

147

5 FACTS ABOUT GIRAFFATITAN

Giraffatitan lived

154 TO 142 MILLION YEARS AGO. #0619

Giraffatitan was a huge **23-metre-long** stout-legged dinosaur. #0620

An incredible **34 individual *Giraffatitan*** fossils were found at a site in **Tanzania, Africa.** #0621

GIRAFFATITAN was discovered between 1909 and 1912, but was named *Brachiosaurus* by mistake. #0622

148

Giraffatitan means **"TITANIC GIRAFFE".** #0623

Gorgosaurus lived **75 MILLION YEARS AGO.** #0624

It may have been an early relative of **TYRANNOSAURUS REX.** #0625

The **fossilized tooth** of one *Gorgosaurus* has been found embedded in another *Gorgosaurus* jaw. They had **probably been fighting.** #0626

Gorgosaurus' **scales were so small that its skin was almost smooth.** #0627

Scientists found the fossil skeleton of one *Gorgosaurus* that had lived for months or even years with **FRACTURES, BROKEN RIBS,** an **INFECTED JAW** and possibly a **BRAIN TUMOUR!** #0628

149

Hadrosaurus lived **78 TO 74 MILLION YEARS AGO.** #0629

Hadrosaurus was 9 METRES LONG and could stand on either two or four legs. #0630

Hadrosaurus fossils were discovered way back in 1838. #0631

It was the **first dinosaur** to be identified from a fossil skeleton in the **United States.** #0632

Hadrosaurus sometimes **ate rotting wood,** probably to consume the fungi and insects the wood contained. #0633

In 1868, it became the **FIRST DINOSAUR SKELETON EVER DISPLAYED.** #0634

150

Herrerasaurus was one of the earliest meat-eating dinosaurs to walk the planet – **231 MILLION YEARS AGO.** #0635

At the time of *Herrerasaurus*, dinosaurs were not the **TOP PREDATORS:** it would have had to run away from the giant forerunners of crocodiles. #0637

Herrerasaurus fossils have been found in Argentina's "Valley of the Moon" – a strange, barren place with a moonscape setting. #0636

Hererrasaurus walked on its **hind legs** and had **powerful, grasping CLAWED HANDS.** #0638

Its blade-like teeth were SHARP AND POINTED. #0639

Herrerasaurus was **3 TO 4 METRES LONG.** #0640

A hinge in its lower jaw helped it to keep a **FIRM GRIP ON STRUGGLING PREY.** #0641

FACTS ABOUT
8 IGUANODON

Iguanodon lived about
125 MILLION YEARS AGO. #0642

One of the most **successful dinosaurs,** *Iguanodon* lived in what is now Europe.
#0643

It was one of the **FIRST** non-bird dinosaurs ever **IDENTIFIED** from fossils and, in 1825, the **SECOND** to be given a formal name. #0644

Its name means
"IGUANA TOOTH". #0645

Iguanodon's teeth resemble those of an iguana (a type of lizard), but the dinosaur was

MUCH BIGGER

at about 10 metres long.

#0646

Mary Ann Mantell found some of *Iguanodon*'s fossil teeth in 1822.

#0647

The greatest number of *Iguanodon* fossils, **an AMAZING 35 to 40 skeletons,** was found in a Belgian coal mine in 1878.

#0648

Iguanodon could easily walk either on

TWO LEGS OR FOUR.

#0649

153

Mei lived around

125 MILLION YEARS AGO. #0650

Mei was discovered in **China, in 2004.** #0651

A fossil skeleton of *Mei* was found with its head tucked under its "wing", like a resting bird.

#0652

Mei was a feathered dinosaur with large eyes and a retractable claw on each foot.

#0653

A small dinosaur, *Mei* was about the **size** of a **duck.** #0654

The living dinosaur may have been asleep when it was

KILLED BY POISONOUS GAS

from a volcano and

BURIED in ASH. #0655

Nothosaurus lived
40 TO 210 MILLION YEARS AGO.
#0656

Nothosaurus probably **hunted shoals** of small **fish.** #0657

It was a
TRIASSIC SEA REPTILE.
#0658

A **sleek swimmer**, Nothosaurus **swam** the seas around what is now **Asia, North Africa** and **Europe.** #0659

Nothosaurus had
WEBBED TOES.
#0660

Nothosaurus' long teeth fitted neatly together with its mouth closed. #0661

NOTHOSAURUS used its tail, legs and feet to steer its 4-metre-long body through water. #0662

10 FACTS ABOUT
OVIRAPTOR

Oviraptor lived about
85 TO 75 MILLION YEARS AGO.
#0663

A fossilized *Oviraptor* was found in the **Gobi Desert** in 1924.
#0664

OVIRAPTOR WAS A SMALL DINOSAUR. IT WAS ONLY
2 metres long.
#0665

Oviraptor could **run 64 kilometres per hour** on its **two long legs**.
#0666

Oviraptor is only known from just **one** main **fossil specimen.** #0667

The *Oviraptor* fossil had a **crushed skull.** A *Protoceratops* may have caused this injury as many *Protoceratops* fossils were found nearby.
#0668

Oviraptor's **parrot-like head** had a **toothless beak** but

POWERFUL CRUSHING JAWS.

#0669

Its **beak** may have been used to **break open clam shells.**

#0670

The small **crest** on its **snout** may have **ATTRACTED** females.

#0671

Scientists think that *Oviraptor* probably had feathers like its close relative, *Citipati*.

#0672

157

6 FACTS ABOUT PACHYRHINOSAURUS

In the early 1970s, a teacher in Canada discovered a site with **hundreds** of fossil *Pachyrhinosaurus* bones from **25 to 30 individual dinosaurs.** #0673

Pachyrhinosaurus measured up to **8 METRES** in length and weighed **4 TONNES.** #0675

A herd of rhinoceros-like *Pachyrhinosaurus* may have **died in a flood 73 million years ago.** #0674

Pachyrhinosaurus is thought to have had **POOR HEARING.** #0676

Its **stubby teeth** were packed tightly together, slicing through plants like **pairs of scissors.** #0677

Pachyrhinosaurus is often found near fossils of the **duck-billed dinosaur *Edmontosaurus*** – this may suggest that their herds travelled together. #0678

Parasaurolophus lived
in what is now North America
70 TO 65 MILLION YEARS AGO. #0679

Parasaurolophus grew up to
12 metres long and
was **2.8 metres high** at the hips. #0680

Parasaurolophus had a
1.8-metre, hollow,
bony crest that was **LONGER
than the rest of its SKULL.**
#0681

Parasaurolophus'
hollow **crest** might
have been used
in courtship
displays or for
making sounds.
#0682

It had a **powerful, pointed
tail** and **scaly, pebbly skin.**
#0683

9 FACTS ABOUT PROTOCERATOPS

Protoceratops lived **75 MILLION YEARS AGO.**
#0684

Protoceratops was a **plant eater** about the size of a **sheep.**
#0685

In 1922, an expedition looking for **early human fossils** in the Gobi Desert, Mongolia, discovered the **first Protoceratops.**
#0686

Protoceratops was one of the **first dinosaurs** to be discovered by its **footprints.**
#0687

In legends, **a griffin** is said to be **lion-sized** with **big claws** and a **beak.** The legend may have been inspired by ancient **Protoceratops** discoveries.
#0688

Protoceratops laid 12 to 15 eggs in its nest. Fossilized **Protoceratops** eggs have been found laid in a spiral pattern.

#0689

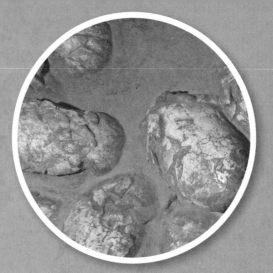

PROTOCERATOPS' JAWS WERE MUSCULAR AND PACKED FULL OF TEETH ABLE TO CHEW TOUGH VEGETATION.

#0690

Some *Protoceratops* had small frills, but others had **ENORMOUS FRILLS** **nearly half the length of their skull.** #0691

Scientists do not know whether **male** and **female** **Protoceratops** had different **frills,** or whether they have identified a **different type** of dinosaur.

#0692

161

8 FACTS ABOUT QUETZALCOATLUS

Quetzalcoatlus is one of the **last-known pterosaurs** that survived to the very end of the Cretaceous, **66 MILLION YEARS AGO.**

#0693

It had two light yet enormous **5-metre-long wings.**

#0694

Like today's owls and eagles, it probably had **excellent eyesight** and could **spot prey** from **high** up in the **air.**

#0695

It was one of the **LARGEST FLYING ANIMALS** ever to exist.

Quetzalcoatlus could glide **HIGH UP** in the air at **3000 to 4500 METRES,** and **SPEED** along at **120 kilometres per hour,** only occassionally flapping its wings.

#0697

When it landed and stood up on its **3-metre-long legs,** it looked a bit like a modern-day giraffe.

#0698

Quetzalcoatlus probably **hunted land animals,** including small dinosaurs.

#0699

Some scientists wonder whether *Quetzalcoatlus* used its **strong front leg muscles** to vault into flight.

#0700

163

12 FACTS ABOUT RAPTORS

Raptors were a group of **two-legged, meat-eating dinosaurs** with **feathered arms.** The scientific name for raptors is **DROMAEOSAURS.**

#0701

Scientists think that most adult raptors were **covered with feathers,** just like the hatchlings and juveniles were.

#0702

VELOCIRAPTOR lived **75 MILLION YEARS AGO.**

#0703

Microraptor lived **120 million years ago.**

#0704

Some raptors had a **HUGE, 22-centimetre-long,** curved **CLAW** on each hind foot.

#0705

MICRORAPTOR had **long feathers** on both its legs AND arms. It was a good glider, but its muscles were probably not strong enough to fly well. #0706

Changyuraptor lived **125 million years ago.** #0707

At just over **1 metre long,** *Changyuraptor* is the **BIGGEST** of all four-winged dinosaurs. #0708

Changyuraptor had **30-CENTIMETRE-LONG TAIL FEATHERS** – the longest of any dinosaur. #0709

Utahraptor lived **126 million years ago.** #0710

Utahraptor was probably warm-blooded, which means it created its own body heat instead of relying on heat from the Sun. #0711

Named after the state of Utah, United States, where it was discovered, *Utahraptor* was the LARGEST RAPTOR dinosaur that ever lived. #0712

9 FACTS ABOUT SAUROPOSEIDON

Sauroposeidon was a giant sauropod dinosaur that lived **110 million** years ago. #0713

SAUROPOSEIDON lived by river deltas on the shores of the Gulf of Mexico, United States. #0714

SAUROPOSEIDON'S thigh bones are the **longest** of any dinosaur. #0715

Although **SAUROPOSEIDON'S** bones were big, they were full of tiny air pockets, which made them light. #0716

When fossil bones of **SAUROPOSEIDON** were first discovered in 1994, they were thought to be fossil **tree trunks!** #0717

166

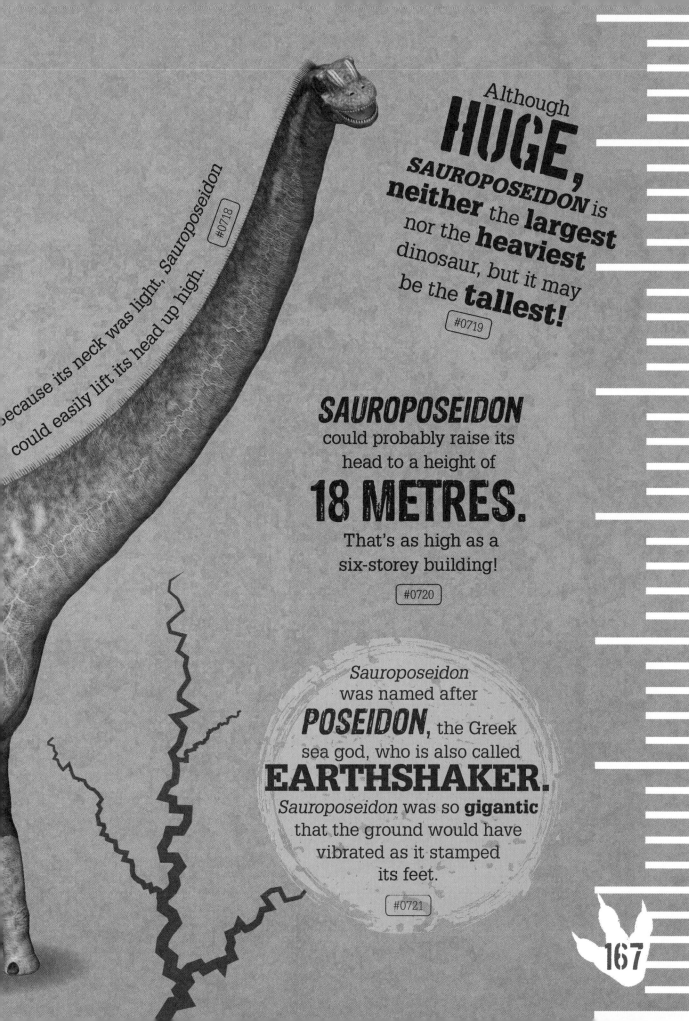

Although **HUGE**, SAUROPOSEIDON is **neither** the **largest** nor the **heaviest** dinosaur, but it may be the **tallest!**

#0719

... because its neck was light, Sauroposeidon could easily lift its head up high.

#0718

SAUROPOSEIDON could probably raise its head to a height of **18 METRES.** That's as high as a six-storey building!

#0720

Sauroposeidon was named after **POSEIDON,** the Greek sea god, who is also called **EARTHSHAKER.** *Sauroposeidon* was so **gigantic** that the ground would have vibrated as it stamped its feet.

#0721

167

9 FACTS ABOUT SPINOSAURUS

Spinosaurus was a meat-eating dinosaur that lived 110 to 95 million years ago. #0722

Spinosaurus is the largest known land predator **of all time.** #0723

The first Spinosaurus fossil was found more than **100 years** ago, but a new fossil was discovered in 2013! #0724

The biggest **SPINOSAURUS** fossil was discovered in the Sahara Desert, Morocco. #0725

SPINOSAURUS had a **crocodile-like snout, paddle-like feet** and **curved, blade-like claws** that hooked into its prey and sliced it up. #0726

SPINOSAURUS was as long as **two** buses! It was nearly 3 metres longer than any known **TYRANNOSAURUS REX.** #0727

SPINOSAURUS had a tall sail on its back.
#0728

SPINOSAURUS lived in swamp areas and probably hunted prehistoric crocodilians and fish.
#0729

Spinosaurus is probably the **FIRST** dinosaur identified as being able to swim.
#0730

169

6 FACTS ABOUT STEGOSAURUS

STEGOSAURUS roamed Earth **155 to 150 million** years ago in the late Jurassic. #0731

Stegosaurus lived in what is now modern-day western North America and Europe. #0732

STEGOSAURUS was the size of a **BUS** and had flat plates along its back. #0733

Stegosaurus held its tail high off the ground, but its head was held **LOW DOWN.** #0734

Stegosaurus weighed **4.5 TONNES,** which is heavier than **six** cows! #0736

Stegosaurus ambled along slowly, eating **bushes** and **shrubs.** #0735

TRICERATOPS lived in the late Cretaceous around 68 to 66 million years ago. #0737

Triceratops' **ENORMOUS** skull, including its frill, could measure more than **2.1 metres** wide! #0738

TRICERATOPS was **9 metres** long and weighed **6** to **12 TONNES.** #0739

Fossilized **TRICERATOPS** skulls are highly sought-after and are bought for **hundreds of thousands of dollars** by dinosaur fans or museum collectors when auctioned. #0740

171

9 FACTS ABOUT TROODON

Troodon lived **74 to 66** million years ago. #0741

Troodon lived in what is now the **UNITED STATES.** #0742

Two-metre-long **TROODON** was a fast runner. It reached speeds of **40** kilometres per hour. #0743

TROODON LOOKED LIKE A BIRD AND MIGHT HAVE HAD **COLOURFUL FEATHERS.** #0744

TROODON was **THREE** times heavier than **VELOCIRAPTOR** and **TWICE** its height! #0745

TROODON means "WOUNDING TOOTH".

Its teeth were **curved, very sharp** and **saw-edged!** #0746

Troodon had grasping hands and one LARGE CLAW on the second toe of each foot. #0747

TROODON laid its teardrop-shaped eggs in a nest. #0748

It is probable that male **TROODON** dinosaurs, rather than females, sat on the eggs in a nest and kept them warm! #0749

10 FACTS ABOUT TYRANNOSAURUS REX

Tyrannosaurus rex walked the Earth **67 to 66 million** years ago. #0750

Tyrannosaurus rex lived in what is now North America. #0751

Its jaws were so **POWERFUL** that *Tyrannosaurus rex* could slice right through its prey's head. #0752

Tyrannosaurus rex belonged to a dinosaur group called **TYRANNOSAURIDAE,** which also included: **ALBERTOSAURUS, ALECTROSAURUS, ALIORAMUS, DASPLETOSAURUS, EOTYRANNUS, GORGOSAURUS, NANOTYRANNUS, PRODEINODON** and **TARBOSAURUS.** #0753

Its **BITE** had about three times the force of the bite of a **GREAT WHITE SHARK!** #0754

174

TYRANNOSAURUS REX was right at the **TOP** of the food chain – no predators dared to take it on! `#0755`

If prey bitten by *Tyrannosaurus rex* didn't die, it would have been left with **wounds** infected by **bacteria** that would kill it. `#0757`

Tyrannosaurus rex probably had very **BAD BREATH!** Pieces of dead meat may have got stuck in its teeth and would have **rotted** and **SMELLED TERRIBLE!** `#0756`

Traces of proteins in **TYRANNOSAURUS REX** bone closely match those of **CHICKENS!** `#0758`

Some **TYRANNOSAURUS REX** bones contain *Tyrannosaurus rex* tooth marks! This suggests it was either a **CANNIBAL** or fought with those of its own species for the attention of females. `#0759`

9 FACTS ABOUT YANGCHUANOSAURUS

YANGCHUANOSAURUS lived 160 to 155 million years ago, in the mid to late Jurassic.

#0760

Yangchuanosaurus was a large, powerful **MEAT EATER** that grew up to 9 metres long.

#0761

Yangchuanosaurus lived in what is now **CHINA.**

#0762

YANGCHUANOSAURUS had **BONY RIDGES** on top of its snout.

#0763

Its tail made up half its length.

#0764

Its huge skull grew up to **1 METRE** long.

#0765

YANGCHUANOSAURUS was similar in looks and size to the much better-known dinosaur, *Allosaurus.*

#0767

A construction worker in Sichuan Province, China, unearthed the first *Yangchuanosaurus* in the 1970s.

#0766

Only **two** main fossil skeletons of **YANGCHUANOSAURUS** have **ever** been found.

#0768

YUNNANOSAURUS lived **205 to 190 million years** ago, in the early Jurassic.

#0769

TWENTY YUNNANOSAURUS fossil skeletons have been discovered!

#0770

YUNNANOSAURUS was a long-necked plant eater that roamed what is now **China.**

#0771

YUNNANOSAURUS was first named in 1942.

#0772

YUNNANOSAURUS HAD MORE THAN 60 SPOON-SHAPED TEETH.

#0773

YUNNANOSAURUS' teeth **sharpened themselves** by rubbing at each other as the dinosaur fed.

#0774

YUNNANOSAURUS was named after Yunnan Province, China, where it was first found.

#0775

Yunnanosaurus weighed up to **1 TONNE.**

#0776

Yunnanosaurus grew up to 7 metres long.

#0777

177

9 FACTS ABOUT FLYING REPTILES

In 2014, a large fossil site was discovered in **BRAZIL**. It contained at least **47 PTEROSAUR** skeletons, now called **CAIUAJARA.** #0778

CAIUAJARA

lived **85 million** years ago and had a head shaped like an old-fashioned **admiral's hat.**

#0779

RHAMPHORHYNCHUS was a pterosaur that lived 150 million years ago. #0780

RHAMPHORHYNCHUS

had small legs, which probably made it a poor runner.

#0781

RHAMPHORHYNCHUS

caught prey in the water by snapping shut its needle-like teeth and then tossing the meal into its throat pouch, just like a modern-day pelican. #0782

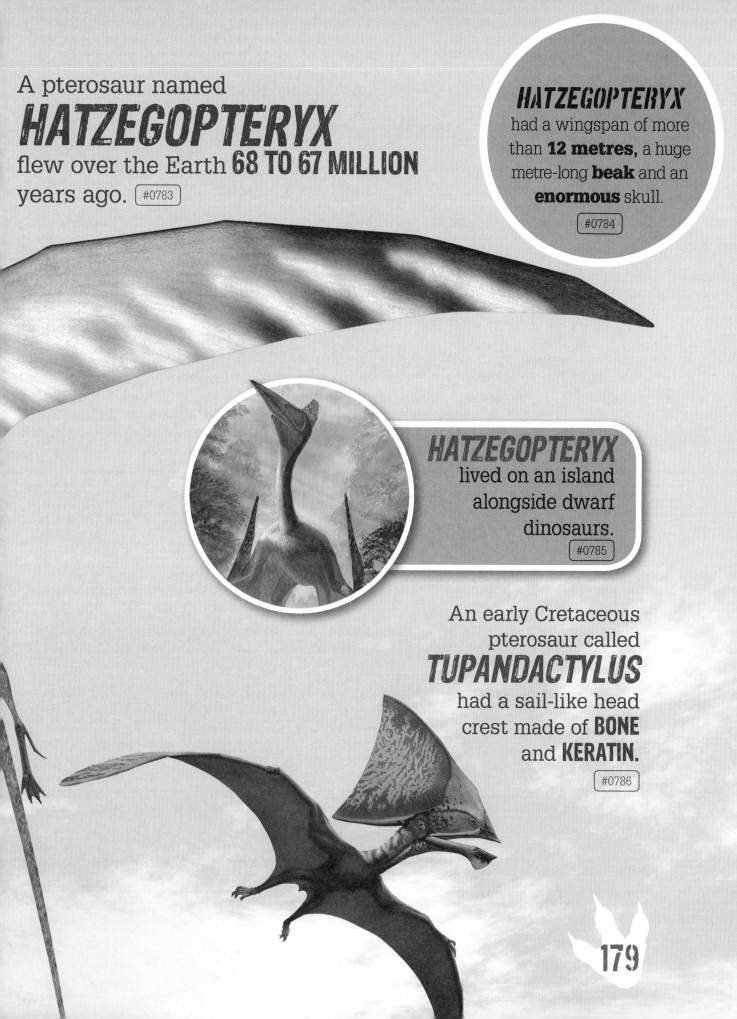

A pterosaur named
HATZEGOPTERYX
flew over the Earth **68 TO 67 MILLION** years ago. #0783

HATZEGOPTERYX
had a wingspan of more than **12 metres**, a huge metre-long **beak** and an **enormous** skull. #0784

HATZEGOPTERYX
lived on an island alongside dwarf dinosaurs. #0785

An early Cretaceous pterosaur called
TUPANDACTYLUS
had a sail-like head crest made of **BONE** and **KERATIN**. #0786

EXTREME PREHISTORIC FACTFILE

Dinosaurs with the **LARGEST CLAWS** included…

…**MEGARAPTOR, THERIZINOSAURUS, BARYONYX, DEINOCHEIRUS** and **SEGNOSAURUS.**

#0787

The pliosaur with the **LARGEST** appetite, swallowing **all** that swam in its way, was **KRONOSAURUS.** It ate large fish, turtles and reptiles.

#0788

#0789

Two of the **MOST FEARSOME PREDATORS** included **SPINOSAURUS** and **MAPUSAURUS.**

SHANTUNGOSAURUS is the **LARGEST** duck-billed dinosaur so far discovered.

#0790

Two of the **BIGGEST PLIOSAURS** ever were **LIOPLEURODON** – a fierce marine predator at **6 to 11** metres long – and **KRONOSAURUS** at **9 to 10** metres long.

#0791

Some of the **SMALLEST** non-bird dinosaurs included *Compsognathus, Microraptor,* and *Mei.*

#0792

Predator X, now officially named *PLIOSAURUS FUNKEI,* was a vast pliosaur with one of the **MOST POWERFUL PREHISTORIC BITES** – four times stronger than *TYRANNOSAURUS REX!*

#0793

A dinosaur with one of the **MOST DIFFICULT NAMES** to say is *EUSTREPTOSPONDYLUS*. It is pronounced "yoo-STREP-toe-spon-DIE-lus".

#0794

Some of the **most well-armoured** dinosaurs included *ANKYLOSAURUS, KENTROSAURUS, EUOPLOCEPHALUS* and *SAUROPELTA*.

#0795

One of the **most well-protected** dinosaurs and the **most well-recognized** was *TRICERATOPS*, with its **MIGHTY ARMOUR.**

#0796

The most **GIGANTIC MEAT EATERS** included *CARCHARODONTOSAURUS*, which is closely related to *GIGANOTOSAURUS.*

#0797

Some of the most **gentle** giant browsers were *DIPLODOCUS* and *APATOSAURUS.*

#0798

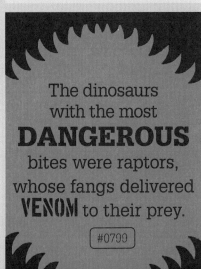

The dinosaurs with the most **DANGEROUS** bites were raptors, whose fangs delivered **VENOM** to their prey.

#0799

EXTINCTION AND BEYOND

Sixty-six million years ago, the world of the dinosaurs changed **FOREVER!** #0800

CHAPTER 7

11 FACTS ABOUT MASS EXTINCTIONS

There have been **FIVE MAJOR** mass extinction events in Earth's history: two during the age of the dinosaurs; a small one at the end of the Triassic; and a larger one at the end of the Cretaceous. #0802

A mass extinction is an event during which a large number of species die out in a short period of time. #0801

At the end of the Cretaceous, *66 MILLION YEARS AGO,* a **mass extinction** killed off the non-bird dinosaurs. #0803

Sixty-six million years ago, three-quarters of plant and animal species **disappeared.** #0804

In the Cretaceous extinction, **ammonites**, countless **flowering plants** and **pterosaurs** perished. #0805

Some **INSECTIVORES** and **OMNIVORES** (creatures that ate almost anything) survived the mass extinction at the end of the Cretaceous, perhaps because there was more for them to eat. #0806

184

At the end of the Cretaceous, most land animals weighing more than

40 KILOGRAMS

died. **BIG** animals need **LOTS** of food and most of their food had **vanished.** #0807

Some **BIRDS** (also called **avian dinosaurs**) were **not** killed in the mass extinction. If they had been, they would **not** be around today! #0808

Big marine reptiles, such as MOSASAURS, PLESIOSAURS and PLIOSAURS, disappeared from the oceans in the mass extinction, 66 million years ago. #0809

More than **80 per cent** of Cretaceous **turtle** species **survived** the mass extinction. #0810

There were **more Cretaceous** survivors in the **sea** and in **fresh water** than on land. #0811

185

THE END OF THE DINOSAUR AGE

Many scientists think that a **massive** meteorite slammed into Earth, **66 million years ago,** ending the reign of the non-bird dinosaurs. #0812

METEORITES can be small or HUGE. #0814

A **METEORITE** is a piece of rock that travels from space and hits the Earth. #0813

Around **66 MILLION YEARS AGO,** the meteorite that hit Earth created the **Chicxulub crater** in **Mexico.** #0815

The **CHICXULUB CRATER** was discovered in the late 1970s. #0816

The **Chicxulub crater** cannot be seen. It was discovered by studying Earth's magnetism and rocks, and by oil-well drilling. #0817

The Chicxulub crater is more than **180 kilometres wide** and **20 kilometres deep.** The meteorite that caused it must have been at least **10 kilometres wide.**

#0818

The meteorite must have been travelling **120 times faster** than an aeroplane!

#0819

IRIDIUM is a metal found in meteorites. There is a layer of iridium on Earth that is **66 million years old** – formed by the meteorite that collided with Earth.

#0820

When a space object hits Earth, glassy, rocky particles form, called **tektites.** Scientists have found **66-million-year-old** tektites, which they believe were created by the meteorite.

#0821

187

FACTS ABOUT
8 THE DEADLY IMPACT

When the meteorite hit **EARTH**, the explosion would have created a **BILLION** times **MORE ENERGY** than the atom bombs dropped during World War II. #0822

Where the **METEORITE** hit Earth, the sky would have turned **RED HOT** for hours.

#0823

In the crater's **impact area**, the surface of the Earth **baked** as if it was in an oven. #0824

The meteorite **IMPACT** would have been felt around the whole world.

#0825

TOXIC GASES from the explosion filled the air, and **ACID RAIN** poured down on the dinosaurs.

#0826

The sea would have risen up into terrifying **MEGA-TSUNAMIS** flooding the land.

#0827

WILD FIRES raged on the land, **BURNING TREES, PLANTS and ANIMALS,** including **DINOSAURS.**

#0828

SHOCK WAVES from the meteorite impact caused **earthquakes!**

#0829

8 FACTS ABOUT THE LAST DAYS OF THE DINOSAURS

When the sun was blocked out, plants **died** because they needed **sunlight** to survive. #0831

Life after the meteorite impact was **dark.** Clouds of **debris, dust** and **ash** blotted out the sun for months. #0830

WITH HARDLY ANY SUNLIGHT, TEMPERATURES WOULD HAVE PLUMMETED – DINOSAURS COULD NOT SURVIVE THESE CHANGES. #0832

Plant-eating dinosaurs, such as huge **20-tonne titanosaurs,** would have died out – they needed to eat **HUNDREDS** of kilograms of vegetation every day and struggled to find a meal. #0833

The meteorite impact triggered **VOLCANIC ERUPTIONS**. Ash blocked out the sun and contributed to the mass extinction.

#0834

A meteorite impact may have caused the **sea levels** to change, destroying large areas of **DINOSAUR HABITAT**.

#0835

Mighty tyrannosaurs and other meat eaters had very little to eat once **VAST** numbers of plant-eating animals had died out.

#0836

The movement of the **GREAT PLATES** that make up **EARTH'S SURFACE** could have also changed the climate and helped to **kill** off the big land **dinosaurs**.

#0837

191

8 FACTS ABOUT MASS EXTINCTION SURVIVORS

When the meteorite struck Earth, some underwater **sea, river** and **lake** creatures were protected from the impact. #0838

Reptiles, including snakes, lizards, crocodilians and turtles, **SURVIVED** the mass extinction when the non-bird dinosaurs and other animals were **KILLED.**
#0839

THE ONLY PLANTS TO SURVIVE WERE THOSE THAT WERE ABLE TO COPE WITH THE NEW **COLDER CLIMATE.**
#0840

Amphibians such as salamanders and frogs survived the MASS EXTINCTION.
#0841

192

THE ONLY DINOSAUR SURVIVORS WERE BIRDS.

#0842

FISH, STARFISH and **SEA URCHINS** survived the mass extinction.

#0843

Mammals **thrived** once there were no dinosaurs around to compete for **land and food.**

#0844

After the non-bird dinosaurs became **EXTINCT, mammals** became the **dominant** land animals.

#0845

193

DINOSAUR DISCOVERERS
FACTFILE

William Buckland was one of the first people to ever name a dinosaur. He named **MEGALOSAURUS** in 1824.
#0846

Richard Owen, born in **1804,** was a clever **palaeontologist, biologist** and **anatomist.**
#0847

Gideon Mantell was the world's first **DINOSAUR HUNTER.** In 1822, he was the first person to identify a dinosaur **tooth.**
#0848

Richard Owen realized that one fossil group, including **MEGALOSAURUS** and **IGUANODON,** all had column-like upright legs, not sprawling reptile legs.
#0849

Richard Owen was the **youngest ever** member of the **Zoological Society of London** in 1830.
#0850

Richard Owen announced that the fossil bones he was examining were NOT LIZARDS AT ALL but something new – DINOSAURS.
#0851

In 1842, Richard Owen gave the name **DINOSAURIA** to the strange fossils he was studying.
#0852

In the 19th century, Richard Owen studied newly discovered **FOSSIL REPTILES** in Britain.
#0853

Today's birds are dinosaurs, so even the BALD EAGLE (the United States' national symbol) and the ROBIN belong to dinosauria.
#0854

As well as dinosaurs, Richard Owen studied **GIANT MOAS**, **KIWIS**, **AFRICAN LUNGFISH**, **GORILLAS** and the **DODO** (an extinct bird).

#0855

Richard Owen gave biology lessons to the children of Britain's QUEEN VICTORIA.

#0856

Richard Owen noticed that an **IGUANODON** tooth had a totally different structure from an **IGUANA** (lizard) tooth.

#0857

It was Richard Owen's

GREAT RIVAL,

Thomas Huxley, who began to see the **links** between **dinosaurs** and **birds.**

#0858

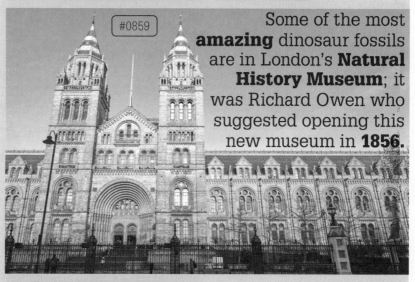

#0859

Some of the most **amazing** dinosaur fossils are in London's **Natural History Museum**; it was Richard Owen who suggested opening this new museum in **1856.**

The palaeontologist **Robert Bakker** was one of the first to suggest that some dinosaurs had **feathers.**

#0860

In 1878, coal miners in Belgium discovered the remains of more than **30 DINOSAURS** in a deep ravine. **Louis Dollo** spent most of his life putting the skeletons **back together.**

#0861

Owen worked hard his whole life until the age of 85. #0862

Paul Sereno travels the world looking for **dinosaur fossils.** He found skeletons of **HERRERASAURUS** and **EORAPTOR** in South America and **AFROVENATOR, DELTADROMEUS, SUCHOMIMUS** and **JOBARIA** in Africa.

#0863

FOSSILS AND DISCOVERY

**People did not
know that fossils were
ANCIENT until the 1800s.**

#0864

CHAPTER 8

14 FACTS ABOUT DINOSAUR FOSSILS

A fossil is the remains or **IMPRESSION** of a **PREHISTORIC** plant or animal, such as...

...a **DINOSAUR**, preserved in rock for many **thousands** or **millions of years.**
#0865

It was **very rare** for a dead dinosaur to turn into a fossil.
#0866

For a fossil to form, the first step was for the body of a creature to become buried by **SAND, MUD** or **SILT.** #0867

Hard dinosaur parts that turned into fossils included **teeth, claws, horns, shells, droppings** and **bones.** #0868

SOFT BODY PARTS OF A DEAD DINOSAUR WERE SOMETIMES EATEN OR JUST ROTTED AWAY. #0869

If hard dinosaur parts were buried by mud or silt, this soft rock eventually became **very hard.**
#0870

198

Sometimes buried dinosaur bones were replaced **particle** by **particle** with **ROCK.**

#0871

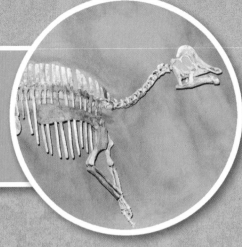

Buried dinosaur bones and other hard parts sometimes **DISSOLVED** over time when they were surrounded by rock, but their **shapes remained.**

#0872

Underground shapes left by dissolved dinosaur bones became **filled** in with water **full** of **minerals.** The water hardened into **EXACTLY** the same **SHAPE** as the skeleton!

#0873

Footprints, scratch marks, tail drag marks and burrows have all been **fossilized.**

#0875

As the top layers of rock wear away over **millions of years,** fossilized dinosaur bones and other hard dinosaur parts gradually **appear** at **EARTH'S SURFACE.**

#0874

Fossils of **DINOSAUR FOOTPRINTS** tell us a lot about how heavy dinosaurs were, how they walked and who was with them at the time.

#0876

The earliest fossils date from **3.5 BILLION** years ago, way before dinosaurs existed.

#0877

The most expensive dinosaur fossil ever sold was a *Tyrannosaurus rex* skeleton named "Sue". It sold for **$8.3 MILLION** in 1997.

#0878

199

7 FACTS ABOUT FOSSIL HUNTING

The name fossil comes from the Latin word **FOSSILIS,** which means "obtained by digging". #0879

FOSSILS are often discovered where land has been disturbed by **construction works** or **coal mining.** #0880

FOSSILS ARE OFTEN FOUND WHEN THERE IS A ROCKFALL IN QUARRIES, ON FARMLAND OR FROM CLIFFS. #0881

Fossils can be found in **MUDSTONE, LIMESTONE** and **SANDSTONE** because these rocks are made of fine grains that settled on the dinosaurs' remains and buried them. #0882

Fossil hunters use **HAMMERS** and **CHISELS**, but the best tool is excellent **EYESIGHT** to spot **shapes** or **textures** in rock. #0883

A fossil may not be the same **colour** as its surroundings if it has a different **mineral content.** #0884

A fossil might be just one tooth or egg, or a vast skeleton, such as that of a gigantic *DREADNOUGHTUS.* #0885

201

11 FACTS ABOUT FAMOUS FOSSIL HUNTERS

Mary Anning was one of the first fossil hunters and found many important fossils in the United Kingdom in the 1820s. #0886

Mary Anning may be the
GREATEST FOSSIL HUNTER
ever known. #0887

In 1903, **William Ferguson** found the first dinosaur fossil in Australia — a claw belonging to a meat-eating **theropod** dinosaur. #0888

In the early 1900s, Barnum Brown was chief fossil hunter for the **American Museum of Natural History.** #0889

Barnum Brown was the first fossil hunter to discover part of a
TYRANNOSAURUS REX
skeleton. #0890

Fossil hunter **Barnum Brown** sometimes used
DYNAMITE
to expose his dinosaur finds. #0891

Edwin H. Colbert discovered DOZENS of dinosaur fossils in the mid-1900s.

#0892

Edwin H. Colbert discovered **LYSTROSAURUS** fossils in Antarctica. This therapsid was also found in what is now South Africa.

#0893

Edwin H. Colbert's fossil discoveries helped prove that **AFRICA** and **ANTARCTICA** used to be joined together as one land mass.

#0894

José F. Bonaparte from South America discovered many dinosaur fossils including **ARGENTINOSAURUS**, one of the **BIGGEST** that ever existed.

#0895

DONG ZHIMING has led numerous fossil-hunting expeditions in China, and has named **20 dinosaurs.** He is called **"China's Mr Dinosaur".** #0896

39 FACTS ABOUT DINOSAUR NAMES

When a new dinosaur is found, the **PALAEONTOLOGIST, RESEARCHER** or its **DISCOVERER** gets to choose its name. #0897

Some dinosaurs are named after the person who paid for the **fossil-hunting expedition.**
#0898

A DINOSAUR MIGHT BE NAMED AFTER THE **PLACE** IT WAS FOUND OR TO HONOUR **SOMEONE** INVOLVED.
#0899

A dinosaur name may describe an **unusual feature** of the dinosaur, such as a big nose, or behaviour, such as being fierce.
#0900

A dinosaur's name can also relate to **when it lived** or to a **famous event.**
#0901

ACANTHOPHOLIS:
spiny scales #0902

APATOSAURUS:
deceptive lizard #0903

BOROGOVIA:
named after the borogoves in Lewis Carroll's poem "Jabberwocky" #0904

BRONTOMERUS:
thunder thigh #0905

BUGENASAURA:
large-cheeked lizard #0906

CARCHARODONTOSAURUS:
shark-tooth lizard #0907

COLEPIOCEPHALE:
knucklehead #0908

CORYTHOSAURUS:
Helmet lizard #0909

CRICHTONSAURUS:
Crichton's lizard (to honor Michael Chrichton, the author of *Jurassic Park*) #0910

CRYOLOPHOSAURUS:
cold-crested lizard #0911

DASPLETOSAURUS:
frightful lizard #0912

DRACOREX:
dragon king #0913

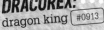

DRYPTOSAURUS:
tearing lizard #0914

EKRIXINATOSAURUS:
explosion-born lizard #0915

EORAPTOR:
dawn thief #0916

GALLIMIMUS:
chicken (or rooster) mimic #0917

HAGRYPHUS:
Ha's griffin (Ha was an Egyptian god) #0918

IRRITATOR CHALLENGERI:
in honour of Professor Challenger in Arthur Conan Doyle's book *The Lost World* #0919

LYTHRONAX:
gore king #0920

MICROPACHYCEPHALOSAURUS:
tiny, thick-headed lizard #0921

NOTHRONYCHUS:
sloth-like claw #0922

ORYCTODROMEUS:
digging runner #0923

QUAESITOSAURUS:
extraordinary lizard #0924

RUGOPS:
wrinkle face #0925

SALTOPUS:
hopping foot #0926

SKORPIOVENATOR:
scorpion hunter #0927

STYGIMOLOCH:
demon from the river Styx #0928

SUPERSAURUS:
super lizard #0929

TARASCOSAURUS:
Spanish dragon lizard #0930

TERATOPHONEUS:
monstrous murderer #0931

TITANOCERATOPS:
titan-horned face #0932

TRICERATOPS:
three-horned face #0933

VELOCIRAPTOR:
speedy thief #0934

VULCANODON:
volcano tooth #0935

13 FACTS ABOUT PREHISTORIC MISTAKES

Fossil dinosaurs are sometimes put together **incorrectly!** #0936

Archaeoraptor was a **fake dinosaur,** made of two separate fossils put together. #0937

Dinosaur illustrations used to be only drawn with green or brown skin. We now know that some non-bird dinosaurs had feathers that were bright red or orange. #0938

Fossil bones from **different** dinosaurs have been put together as **one** dinosaur. #0939

Until very recently, people thought that a **PLESIOSAUR** named Nessie lived in Loch Ness, Scotland. #0940

MEGALOSAURUS was discovered in a quarry in Britain in 1676, but at the time people thought it was a large animal's femur... or a **GIANT'S THIGH!** #0941

STEGOSAURUS was once thought to have a second brain in its rump! #0942

The name **GORGOSAURUS** was "dropped" when its fossils were thought to be a young **ALBERTOSAURUS.** Many years later, fossils proved that these two dinosaurs were different after all, and the name **GORGOSAURUS** was reclaimed! #0943

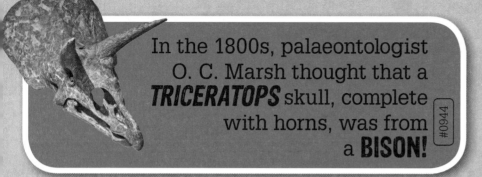

In the 1800s, palaeontologist O. C. Marsh thought that a **TRICERATOPS** skull, complete with horns, was from a **BISON!** #0944

People used to think that dead dinosaurs **EXPLODED** when gas built up inside them. #0945

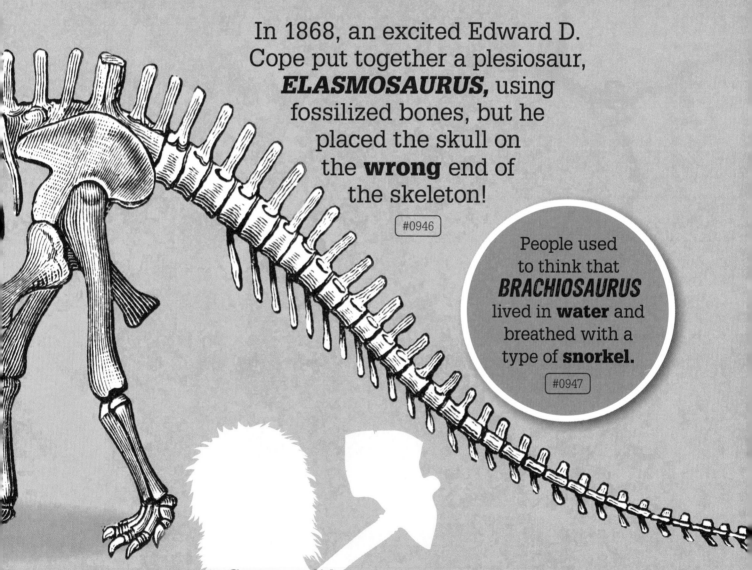

In 1868, an excited Edward D. Cope put together a plesiosaur, **ELASMOSAURUS,** using fossilized bones, but he placed the skull on the **wrong** end of the skeleton! #0946

People used to think that **BRACHIOSAURUS** lived in **water** and breathed with a type of **snorkel.** #0947

Cavemen did **not** fight dinosaurs as shown in many movies and cartoons. There were more than **65.8 MILLION YEARS** between the last dinosaurs and modern humans. #0948

13 FACTS ABOUT MESOZOIC BIRDS

During the Mesozoic Era, small, meat-eating dinosaurs evolved into birds. **All birds are DINOSAURS.**

#0949

Birds have evolved from **avian dinosaurs.**

#0950

All birds have a **beak, wings** and **feathers,** and most can **fly.** This was true during the Mesozoic, and it's still true for birds today.

#0951

Not **all** dinosaurs were birds. Huge *BRACHIOSAURUS* and fierce *TYRANNOSAURUS REX* were **not** birds; they didn't even have wings! These are non-avian or non-bird dinosaurs.

#0952

There was an **incredible** variety of birds in the Cretaceous: birds with **SHORT** tails and **LONG** tails, birds with **MANY** teeth and those with **NO** teeth.

#0953

Some non-bird dinosaurs had **FEATHERS** and even **WINGS,** but parts of their skeletons show they were not quite true birds.

#0954

Powered flight has evolved in at least **FOUR** groups of animals: **INSECTS** then **PTEROSAURS** then **BIRDS** then **BATS.**

#0955

Only 11 or 12 **ARCHAEOPTERYX** specimens have been found and one was a single feather!

#0956

Avian dinosaurs had **large eyes** to help them **HUNT** and **SURVIVE.**

#0957

CONFUCIUSORNIS

was an avian dinosaur, a bird, whose fossils were found in China.

#0958

CONFUCIUSORNIS

lived 125 million years ago!

#0959

CONFUCIUSORNIS

was found in volcanic ash and silt in an ancient lake.

#0960

The non-avian dinosaurs died out in the mass extinction 66 million years ago. Avian dinosaurs survived and gradually **evolved** into the birds we know today.

#0961

209

7 FACTS ABOUT TODAY'S DINOSAURS: BIRDS!

Dinosaur fossils found in China have recently proved that today's birds are not just **similar** to dinosaurs, they **ARE** dinosaurs!

#0962

Birds' skeletons, especially their **arms, wrists** and **hand bones,** link bird dinosaur fossils to **TODAY'S** birds.

#0963

MODERN BIRDS HAVE ADAPTED TO NEARLY EVERY HABITAT ON OUR PLANET.

#0964

MODERN BIRDS RANGE FROM TINY WRENS TO HUGE SEA EAGLES.

#0965

If you ever eat a chicken or an egg, **you are eating a dinosaur!** #0966

The smallest dinosaurs that ever lived are today's **HUMMINGBIRDS!** #0967

The **WANDERING ALBATROSS** has the largest recorded wingspan of any bird alive today. It measures up to **3.5 metres** from wing tip to wing tip.

#0968

FACTS ABOUT
8 NEW DINOSAUR DISCOVERIES

In 2014, Robert Bakker reported that a hole in a fossilized **ALLOSAURUS'** pelvis was probably caused by **STEGOSAURUS' tail spikes**. An abscess shows that the injury became **infected** and probably **killed** the **ALLOSAURUS**.

#0970

A 140-million-year-old fossilized dinosaur tooth found in Malaysia in 2014 belonged to an unnamed brand **NEW** species of bird-hipped dinosaur.

#0969

In 2014, a new dinosaur, **TACHIRAPTOR ADMIRABILIS,** was named.

#0971

TACHIRAPTOR ADMIRABILIS is only the second dinosaur ever found in **Venezuela** and the first meat-eating one.

#0972

In 2014, two **70-million-year-old** *DEINOCHEIRUS MIRIFICUS* skeletons were pieced together from fossils found in the Gobi Desert. #0973

In 2014, a fisherman from Alberta, Canada, hooked an almost **80-million-year-old** dinosaur fossil from the water. It was set in a river boulder. #0975

Recent reports tell us that **11-metre-long** *DEINOCHEIRUS MIRIFICUS* had very long, clawed forearms, a duck-like bill and a humped sail back – but **no teeth!** #0974

Palaeontologists have called *DEINOCHEIRUS* **"wild beyond imagination"** and "a prehistoric mix of horse, ostrich, camel and duck". #0976

213

6 FACTS ABOUT DINOSAUR FIRSTS

The first dinosaur types arrived **240 TO 230 MILLION** years ago, one of the most primitive being **EORAPTOR** from Argentina and Brazil.

#0977

The first **meat-eating** dinosaur was **HERRERASAURUS,** which lived **228** million years ago.

#0978

The first **COMPLETE** dinosaur skeleton discovered was of **HADROSAURUS** and was found by **William Parker Foulke,** in 1858.

#0979

THE **FIRST** SCIENTIST TO CLEARLY REALIZE THAT BIRDS EVOLVED FROM DINOSAURS SUCH AS *DEINONYCHUS* WAS JOHN OSTROM, IN THE 1960S. #0980

The **FIRST** dinosaur finds were described by Chinese historian **Chang Qu** as **"DRAGON BONES"**. They were found in Sichuan, China, more than **2000** years ago. #0981

The **FIRST** dinosaur in space was hadrosaur *MAIASAURA PEEBLESORUM,* in 1985. Astronaut Loren Acton took its bone pieces and eggshell on a SpaceLab 2 mission. #0982

FOSSIL FUN
FACTFILE

Only a **very small** percentage of dinosaurs became **FOSSILS.** #0983

More than 10 new dinosaurs are discovered each year. #0984

If you discover a dinosaur, you are allowed to **CHOOSE ITS NAME!** #0986

Scientists sometimes have just one **DINOSAUR BONE** to try to calculate a dinosaur's size. #0985

Scientists use modern **MEDICAL SCANNERS** to learn more about dinosaur fossils. #0987

In 1853, 21 scientists ate a New Year's Eve banquet **inside** a hollow, concrete **IGUANODON** at London's Crystal Palace. #0988

The fossilized bodies of duck-billed dinosaurs often still had the **skin** wrapped around the **BONES.** #0989

In the nineteenth century, **American pioneers** heading west across America found fossilized bones of great dinosaurs from **LONG AGO.** #0990

Some early **American pioneers** used big fossil dinosaur bones to make **SHELTERS!** #0991

The nation with the biggest number of different types of non-bird dinosaur fossil is the **United States.**

#0992

Great Britain was home to more than 100 non-bird dinosaur species, including ***Megalosaurus, Iguanodon, Neovenator, Eotyrannus,*** and ***Cetiosaurus.***

#0994

Argentina and **Canada** have the third- and fourth-greatest number of types of non-bird dinosaur fossil in the world.

#0993

China has the second-greatest number of types of non-bird dinosaur fossil.

#0995

Professional fossil hunting began in **Great Britain.**

#0996

Great Britain was once part of a **Mesozoic "land bridge"** between North America and Eurasia, over which dinosaurs crossed.

#0997

CHINA and **ARGENTINA** are where most new dinosaur fossil finds are happening.

#0998

The fossil remains of MONSTER-LIKE dinosaurs and flying pterosaurs may have inspired the DRAGON LEGENDS.

#0999

A set of ***SPINOSAURUS*** fossils was unfortunately **destroyed** during **World War II.**

#1000

INDEX

218

221

ACKNOWLEDGEMENTS

t = top, b = bottom, l = left, r = right, c = centre

6–7 Computer Earth/Shutterstock.com, 8–9, 10b, 38–39, 54–55, 88–89, 90–91, 105tr, 169tr, 202c Kostyantyn Ivanyshen/Shutterstock.com, 9b, 14b, 14tr, 27br, 31b, 34, 47b, 49b, 56br, 61c, 67, 69b, 79tr, 86br, 95tr, 95b, 99tl, 112–113, 122–123, 125br, 126–127, 128, 138–139, 146–147, 157r, 162–163, 164–165, 176, 178–179, 181bl, 203b, 215tr Michael Rosskothen/Shutterstock.com, 10t, 147b, 214–215 Lefteris Papaulakis/Shutterstock.com, 11, 12t Designua/Shutterstock, 13, 205br 3Dalia/Shutterstock.com, 14tl TyBy/Shutterstock.com, 15tl alice-photo/Shutterstock.com, 15cl, 15bl, 15br, 42b, 56tr leonello calvetti/Shutterstock.com, 15tr, 16–17, 20–21, 32, 35t, 41, 41t, 57r, 57bl, 58–59, 63b, 68b, 76tl, 76tr, 205t Catmando/Shutterstock.com, 16b Kseniia Romanova/Shutterstock.com, 17t ArtHarbor/Shutterstock.com, 18cr Tribalium/Shutterstock.com, 19tr, 26bc Potapov Alexander/Shutterstock.com, 19c Incredible_movements/Shutterstock.com, 19br kaa67alex/Shutterstock.com, 20t Fricke Studio/Shutterstock.com, 20bl jannoon028/Shutterstock.com, 21tr Elena Kazanskaya/Shutterstock.com, 21cr, 37b, 57tr, 120t, 121c, 123t, 163r ylq/Shutterstock.com, 22bl, 22cr Howard Grey/Getty Images, 22t, 23l(inset), 23br(inset) Yaviki/Shutterstock.com, 22l(inset), 23br(inset) Ksanawo/Shutterstock.com, 22br sunlight77/Shutterstock.com, 22–23, 23r, 23b Ansis Klucis/Shutterstock.com, 24tl Yuriy Priymak/Stocktrek Images/Getty Images, 24bl lantapix/Shutterstock.com, 25tl, 25tr, 25b, 81cr, 99tr, 124bl, 156–157, 173tr, 173br DEA PICTURE LIBRARY/Getty Images, 26–27 abeadev/Shutterstock.com, 26tcl elmm/Shutterstock.com, 26tl Fricke Studio/Shutterstock.com, 26tr alexokokok/Shutterstock.com, 26bl scubaluna/Shutterstock.com, 26br GlebStock/Shutterstock.com, 27tc Steinar/Shutterstock.com, 27l Robert Adrian Hillman/Shutterstock.com, 28–29 Sergey Krasovskiy/Getty Images, 29t, 35b, 40–40t, 41b, 44t, 64t, 91t, 104cl, 125c, 127br Leremy/Shutterstock.com, 30–31, 42c, 46–47, 71cl, 76tc, 76b, 77tl, 125tc, 136–137, 137b, 158, 164b, 166–167, 205ct, 205cb Linda Bucklin/Shutterstock.com, 30tc Fricke Studio/Shutterstock.com, 33t, 50b, 62, 117br, 119b, 149b, 150, 160–161, 172–173, 180br, 205tr Nobumichi Tamura/Stocktrek Images/Getty Images, 33m yyang/Shutterstock.com, 36–37 Sergey Krasovskiy/Getty Images, 37 Ralf Juergen Kraft/Shutterstock.com, 37tr laraslk/Shutterstock.com, 31t, 38t elmm/Shutterstock.com, 39tr Dreamframer/Shutterstock.com, 39b Fricke Studio/Shutterstock.com, 40b IsaArt/Shutterstock.com, 41c Yaviki/Shutterstock.com, 42t maglyvi/Shutterstock.com, 43t Ozja/Shutterstock.com, 43b, 204 DM7/Shutterstock.com, 44b nemlaza/Shutterstock.com, 45t Peter Bull/Getty Images, 45m Nataleana/Shutterstock.com, 45b Sofia Santos/Shutterstock.com, 47t O. Louis Mazzatenta/Getty Images, 47r KoQ Creative/Shutterstock.com, 48t Sergey Krasovskiy/Getty Images, 48b LSkywalker/Shutterstock.com, 49t Vector Icon/Shutterstock.com, 50–51 Donjiy/Shutterstock.com, 51t Valentyna Chukhlyebova/Shutterstock.com, 52–53 Ozja/Shutterstock.com, 53t Valentyna Chukhlyebova/Shutterstock.com, 53m ekler/Shutterstock.com, 53b David Herraez Calzada/Shutterstock.com, 54t Scientifica/Getty Images, 54b gst/Shutterstock.com, 55t seeyou/Shutterstock.com, 56tl, 65b, 98–99, 135, 168–169, 170, 174–175, 181tr, 190–191, 205bl Elenarts/Shutterstock.com, 56m elmm/Shutterstock.com, 57mt dkvektor/Shutterstock.com, 57l Voropaev Vasiliy/Shutterstock.com, 57m Elena Kazanskaya/Shutterstock.com, 57br guysal/Shutterstock.com, 60–61 Wuttichok Painichiwarapun/Shutterstock.com, 60tr Yuriy Priymak/Stocktrek Images/Getty Images, 60b Andreas Meyer/Shutterstock.com, 61br CatbirdHill/Shutterstock.com, 63t Frank Stober/Getty Images, 64–65 Claire McAdams/Shutterstock.com, 64b Peter Minister/Getty Images, 65t TTphoto/Shutterstock.com, 66–66tr Andreas Meyer/Shutterstock.com, 67b Cat_arch_angel/Shutterstock.com, 68–69 Leonello Calvetti/Stocktrek Images/Getty Images, 70–71 George W. Bailey/Shutterstock.com, 70bl Ihnatovich Maryia/Shutterstock.com, 71tr Michele Dessi/Stocktrek Images/Getty Images, 71cr Potapov Alexander/Shutterstock.com, 72t Rob Hainer/Shutterstock.com, 72b SCIEPRO/Getty Images, 73 Lumir Jurka Lumis/Shutterstock.com, 73tr Herschel Hoffmeyer/Shutterstock.com, 74–75 Arthur Dorety/Stocktrek Images/Getty Images, 75tr Colin Keates/Getty Images, 75cl Mark Stevenson/Stocktrek Images/Getty Images, 76–77 ideeone/Getty Images, 77tr Viktorya170377/Shutterstock.com, 77b Jaroslav Moravcik/Shutterstock.com, 78–79 3dmotus/Shutterstock.com, 80–81 Space-kraft/Shutterstock.com, 82–83 Kaidash/Shutterstock.com, 82b Dorling Kindersley/Getty Images, 83tr Gabrielle Hovey/Shutterstock.com, 83c Robert Biedermann/Shutterstock.com 83b Sergey Krasovskiy/Stocktrek Images/Getty Images, 84–85 Aaron Rutten/Shutterstock.com, 85l Jun Mu/Shutterstock.com, 86tl Aron Brand/Shutterstock.com, 86tc gst/Shutterstock.com, 86tr Kayser_999/Shutterstock.com, 86br Tribalium/Shutterstock.com, 86cr fad82/Shutterstock.com, 87tl elm/Shutterstock.com, 87tr Mark Stevenson/Stocktrek Images/Getty Images, 87cl Cat_arch_angel/Shutterstock.com, 87c Martha Marks/Shutterstock.com, 87bc Hein Nouwens/Shutterstock.com, 87br Maks Narodenko/Shutterstock.com, 90b Valentyna Chukhlyebova/Shutterstock.com, 91r wanchai/Shutterstock.com, 91bl lineartestpilot/Shutterstock.com, p92–93, 93tr DM7/Shutterstock.com, 92tr Sofia Santos/Shutterstock.com, 92b Sergey Krasovskiy/Getty Images, 93tl Rodolfo Nogueira/Stocktrek Images/Getty Images, 93cr Nikiteev_Konstantin/Shutterstock.com, 94–95 Yuriy Priymak/Stocktrek Images/Getty Images, 94t Catmando/Shutterstock.com, 96–97 Sergey Krasovskiy/Getty Images, 96b Jim Channell/Getty Images, 98ct Ozja/Shutterstock.com, 98cb Ralf Juergen Kraft/Shutterstock.com, 100–101 Mark Stevenson/Stocktrek Images/Getty Images, 100tr Scientifica/Getty Images, 101tr Andreas Meyer/Shutterstock.com, 101bl yyang/Shutterstock.com, 102bl rudall30/Shutterstock.com, 103br DM7/Shutterstock.com, 104tl HitToon.Com/Shutterstock.com, 104tr Sergey Krasovskiy/Stocktrek Images/Getty Images, 104bl Stefanina Hill/Shutterstock.com, 104bc Pefkos/Shutterstock.com, 104 brt phloem/Shutterstock.com, 104brm Alemon cz/Shutterstock.com, 104brb, 105brtl Alexander Ryabintsev/Shutterstock.com, 105cl Shutterstock.com, 105cr elvil/Shutterstock.com, 105bl Getty Images, 105brl Z-art/Shutterstock.com, 105brbr Lukiyanova Natalia/frenta/Shutterstock.com, 106–107 Mohamad Haghani/Stocktrek Images/Getty Images, 108–109 Elena Duvernay/Stocktrek Images/Getty Images, 108bl Pasko Maksim/Shutterstock.com, 108c Skalapendra/Shutterstock.com, 109br Tomas Smolek/Shutterstock.com, 110–111, 130–131, 132–133, 134, 138b, 140tl , 180tr Catmando/Shutterstock.com, 111tr Ralf Juergen Kraft/Shutterstock.com, 114–115 Science Photo Library - MARK GARLICK/Getty Images, 114bl elm/Shutterstock.com, 114br Shutterstock.com, 116–117 Dave King/Getty Images, 117tr, 124tr maglyvi/Shutterstock.com, 118 Roman Garcia Mora/Stocktrek Images/Getty Images, 119t, 138t Filip Bjorkman/Shutterstock.com, 119c nemlaza/Shutterstock.com, 120–121 Walter Myers/Stocktrek Images/Getty Images, 121t Corey Ford/Stocktrek Images/Getty Images, 124tc 3drenderings/Shutterstock.com, 124br Markus Gann/Shutterstock.com, 129, 140b Leonello Calvetti/Stocktrek Images/Getty Images, 130l mr.Timmi/Shutterstock.com, 131r LEONELLO CALVETTI/Getty Images, 137c mirabile/Shutterstock.com, 141 Tupungato/Shutterstock.com, 142–143 MCT/Contributor/Getty Images, 143tr Jorg Hackemann/Shutterstock.com, 144, 177, 192–193 De Agostini Picture Library/Contributor/Getty Images, 145, 172br Herschel Hoffmeyer/Shutterstock.com, 146bl Benguhan/Shutterstock.com, 147t elm/Shutterstock.com, 148t Ricky Edwards/Shutterstock, 148b Rodolfo Nogueira/Stocktrek Images/Getty Images, 149t Colin Keates/Getty Images, 151 Mohamad Haghani/Stocktrek Images/Getty Images, 152–153, 179c Sergey Krasovskiy/Stocktrek Images/Getty Images, 154 Emily Willoughby/Stocktrek Images/Getty Images, 155 Peter Minister/Getty Images, 159 Mark Stevenson/Stocktrek Images/Getty Images, 160b subarashii21/Shutterstock.com, 160t ArtHeart/Shutterstock.com, 161tr Ken Lucas/Getty Images, 162b Gallinago_media/Shutterstock.com, 163tl Jared Shomo/Shutterstock.com, 166t Anton Foltin/Shutterstock.com, 170br karawan/Shutterstock.com, 171t Ralf Juergen Kraft/Shutterstock.com, 171b David Herraez Calzada/Shutterstock.com, 179b Sergey Krasovskiy/Getty Images, 180tl Andy Crawford/Getty Images, 180c Elle Arden Images/Shutterstock.com, 181c Viktorya170377/Shutterstock.com, 182–183 Esteban De Armas/Shutterstock.com, 184–185 KARSTEN SCHNEIDER/Getty Images, 184l, 216tr weter 777/Shutterstock.com, 185tr Bipsun/Shutterstock.com, 186–187 MARK GARLICK/Getty Images, 186cl eatcute/Shutterstock.com, 188–189 solarseven/Shutterstock.com, 188cl Lukiyanova Natalia/frenta/Shutterstock.com, 189cr Jens Carsten Rosemann/Getty Images, 109bl linagifts/Shutterstock.com, 190tr milo827/Shutterstock.com, 191tr Pablo Hidalgo - Fotos593/Shutterstock.com, 192bl AntiMartina/Shutterstock.com, 192t Studio Barcelona/Shutterstock.com, 194tr file404/Shutterstock.com, 194c Shutterstock.com, 194br Neil Burton/Shutterstock.com, 194bl Teguh Mujiono/Shutterstock.com, 195tl AuntSpray/Shutterstock.com, 195tr Joseph Calev/Shutterstock.com, 195c Nando Machado/Shutterstock.com, 196–197 Marcio Jose Bastos Silva/Shutterstock.com, 198 MarijaPilTponyte/Shutterstock.com, 199tr BG6English School/Getty Images, 202b kontur-vid/Shutterstock.com, 203t Bob Landry/Contributor/Getty Images, 206–207 ivan-96/Getty Images, 207t Marques/Shutterstock.com, 209tr Natursports/Shutterstock.com, 209bl Dorling Kindersley/Getty Images, 210–211 Paul Marto/EyeEm/Getty Images, 210b Gallinago_media/Shutterstock.com, 212–213 Mark Stevenson/Stocktrek Images/Getty Images, 213b Jeffrey L. Osborn/Getty Images, 214b CatbirdHill/Shutterstock.com, 215b IhorZigor/Shutterstock.com, 216c iunewind/Shutterstock.com, 216bl Andrew Chin/Shutterstock.com, 216br h3c7or/Shutterstock.com, 217t chrupka/Shutterstock.com, 217bl Coneyl Jay/Getty Images, 217br vectorOK/Shutterstock.com